British Politics
Unravelled

British Politics Unravelled

A Politico's Guide

Giles Edwards

POLITICO'S

First published in 2006
Politico's Publishing, an imprint of
Methuen Publishing Limited
11–12 Buckingham Gate
London
SW1E 6LB

10 9 8 7 6 5 4 3 2 1

Typeset by SX Composing DTP, Rayleigh, Essex
Printed and bound in Great Britain by Bookmarque Ltd, Croydon,
Surrey

Methuen Publishing Limited Reg. No. 3543167

A CIP catalogue record for this book is available from the British
Library.

ISBN-10 1 84275 152 2
ISBN-13 978 1 84275 152 7

Contents

Foreword

by Nick Robinson

Declaring that you're fascinated in politics can sometimes feel like admitting that you talk to the trees or have a secret perversion. It's become fashionable to parade disdain for politicians and all their works. And yet conversation down the Dog and Duck, in the office canteen or in front of the telly so often revolves around choices about how our lives are governed – in other words, around political choices made by politicians. Should you be allowed to smoke in the bar or down the club? That's a political decision. Should you be able to call Islam a wicked religion or for those who insult the prophet to be punished or even killed? That's a debate that begins with a political decision. Should British soldiers fight, kill and die in our name in Iraq or Afghanistan? Once again, it's a political decision. All too often, though, the connection between the issues that provoke the fiercest debates – which fill newspapers and electrify phone-ins – are disconnected from the process that led to those decisions being made.

When someone attempts to make that connection it's often done with a jumble of jargon and Westminster waffle which leaves the casual observer more baffled still. My experience as a broadcaster teaches me that what many people crave is not to share my interest in political trainspotting but to be armed with enough knowledge to empower them to understand who is doing what and why on their behalf. Others with a real interest in politics want to get beyond the inevitably simplified explanations that we can deliver in a two-minute broadcast or a single article in the papers. That's where *British Politics Unravelled* comes in. I heartily recommend it. Its author, Giles Edwards, has time and again helped me try to convey what's going on in the fascinating world of politics to viewers, listeners and readers who are merely lending us their attention for a passing moment.

He has a real grasp of not only how politics works but also how to communicate it to others who do not share his passion. The cynics are always predicting the death of politics or the end of interest in it. I'm not complacent but turnout was up at the last election and the arrival of not one or two but three new party leaders can only help make politics more interesting still – as can this book. Enjoy it.

Acknowledgements

This book, whilst not quite a collaborative effort, could not have been written without the help of many people. The staff of the British Library, and the fine people at the EC representation in London, were particularly helpful, and I really should also thank Tim Berners-Lee, for without the web I don't know where I'd be.

While writing this book, I've also been working on my PhD and want to thank Peter Hennessy and James Ellison for bearing with me while I learned a lesson about what twenty-four hours in a day actually means.

I'm delighted that this book is published by Politico's, who have never been anything other than über-supportive of my efforts. It would never have got going without the help and support of Emma Musgrave and Sean Magee, and would not have been completed without Jonathan Wadman and Alan Gordon Walker. Thanks also to Jon Shipley at the Westminster Bookshop, whose timely intervention was crucial to getting it going in the first place.

The idea first came from my friends, and they have been extremely enthusiastic about it ever since. It's thanks to them that so many of the questions in this book are real questions posed by real people: Sherry Abuel-Ealeh, Dan Bunting, Victoria Halliwell, Sarah Robinson, Karen Salem, Laura Simpson, Jane Sugars, Ian Swarbrick, Katherine Symonds, Thomas Taylor and Haydee Toltz. Thank you so much to all of them for their friendship and continued forbearance!

For help with the answers, I'd have been lost without the assistance of colleagues and friends at the BBC, in particular Peter Barnes, Ruth Cobbe, Michael Cockerell, David Cowling, Peter Hunt, David Jordan and the wonderful Kate Phillips.

My parents have supported me in every endeavour so far, and this time their computer and proofreading skills were, once again, up to the challenge.

But one person above all others has made this book possible. Vinita read it, suggested ideas, helped with answers, put up with my crazy work schedule and kept me sane. She was also kind enough to tell me that the first draft of the first chapter was useless and I should start again. She was right, and this book is much better for her honesty. In the year we will marry and set up home together, it is only right that book should be dedicated to her.

Finally, for all this help the ultimate responsibility does and always should always rest with the author, so if there are faults they are mine, and mine alone.

Giles Edwards
Twickenham, January 2006

Introduction

British politics is a series of fascinating paradoxes. We have one of the oldest democracies in the world, yet we are still 'subjects' of our hereditary Queen rather than 'citizens' of a state. We have a parliament with more members than most, yet its members exercise less power than most. We have the fourth largest economy in the world and a global reach which few countries can match, yet we are always worrying about our place in the world. We have one of the most open and least corrupt political systems in the world, yet are always worrying about how closed politics is, and how corrupt. In recent years, more opportunities to participate and have their say have inspired people to vote less.

Yet politics isn't so hard to understand, or to navigate. Behind all these weird contradictions politics is not some parallel dimension but a world of work like many others. It has more influence over the rest of us, to be sure, but just like everywhere else it has rules and structures, and to understand them is to understand how things get done (and why they sometimes don't).

There are plenty of people around who want to help the public navigate their politics. Journalists often do a good job of explaining what's happening, yet in the daily hustle-bustle they don't always have time to step back and explain how things got to where they are today. Academics, meanwhile, do a good job of explaining the theories and structures, but not such a good job of linking them to daily events. And then there are the politicians themselves. Contrary to popular opinion, they are not all a bunch of self-serving bastards, but watching debates in Parliament or listening to a politician refusing to answer a question on the radio doesn't really help people understand what they're up to. The stories they tell in their memoirs are often very entertaining, but sometimes seem to be more about getting serialised in the *Mail on Sunday* than explaining why things happened the way they did.

This book hopes to cut through all that, ditching the jargon and the unnecessary complexity and answering the important questions instead. It will explain why British politics developed the way it did and how it works now. It's a guide through the pathways of power, from your local council to the Prime Minister's office in No. 10 and the United Nations in New York – what they do, how they do it, and how it affects you.

I think politics is fascinating. I'm passionate about it, perhaps even a bit obsessed. But to gain a good understanding of what's going on, obsession is not required. Instead, rather like surfing, skiing or riding a bicycle, all you need are a few basics at the beginning, and then you can go and do the rest yourself. This book aims to provide those basics: how to get up on the board, how not to fall off the skis, how to keep the bicycle upright. With that in mind, here are some things which underlie everything else in the book.

What makes Britain a democracy?

Britain's democracy is about much more than how our constitution operates or how we choose our leaders. That is why this book covers the role of all sorts of things which lie outside the realm of formal politics – from campaigns such as Make Poverty History to the role of media outlets such as the *Daily Mail* or the BBC. Together, this huge political hinterland is known as 'civil society', and it is as important to the way our society functions as anything in the chapters on Parliament or elections.

Furthermore, this varied and dynamic civil society is one of the ways in which people most often express their political views. When people join the RSPB, when they buy Fair Trade products or volunteer to help their local youth group, they are doing more than just helping that organisation or individual in a direct way. They're building 'social capital', something which makes a stronger society, and they're expressing a political view: making clear that this issue matters to them and that they are prepared to do something about it. Apathy and declining political participation are less obvious if you see how many different ways someone can get involved in politics in Britain's pluralist democracy.

Where's the power?

Many questions in this book are about who has the power to do various things. That is because politics is about the exercise of power – who's got it, how they got it, how they use it, why, and for what. Yet answering these questions is often really difficult, for three reasons:

- The power to take decisions is often shared by lots of different people – sometimes called plurality in decision making.
- Having the 'power' to do something doesn't necessarily make someone 'powerful'. Some Cabinet ministers have more formal powers than the Prime Minister, for example, yet none is as powerful as the PM.
- People in power often feel they don't have very much. Many politicians will tell you so, and one former PM said

> power is 'like a Dead Sea fruit. When you achieve it, there
> is nothing there.'

As well as power, politics is also about balancing priorities. Of
course you'd like to cut taxes, but are you prepared to cut
spending to balance the books? Of course you want to protect
the environment, but are you prepared to force people to use
their cars less? Of course we must tackle pensioner poverty and
give children the best education possible, but how will we pay
for both?

Politics is as complicated as every other realm of life, and this
makes providing simple answers difficult. What's more, even
people working in and around politics disagree about much of
this stuff. Many answers in this book skip over a great deal of
detail to get to the essence of the subject; many others try to
present both sides of the debate fairly.

How can I influence what happens?

Answering this question is one of the reasons I wrote this book.
There are many ways of influencing what happens, but before
you start you need to know who does what, and where and how
they do it. The questions about where the power lies should
provide that information, and then it's possible to figure out how
to make your influence felt.

What do 'left' and 'right' mean?

The terms originated during the French Revolution, when
the republicans in the legislature sat on the left-hand side of the

assembly. Today, the political left generally includes socialists and liberals while the right includes conservatives. But although they're still heavily used, these terms are no longer quite as useful as they once were.

Many people now find it more useful to think of where they sit on two different political spectrums. One is the traditional left–right economic spectrum – do you want taxes to rise or fall, and so on. The other is for social policy, and the two ends are 'libertarian' (live and let live) and 'authoritarian' (we should make laws to gain conformity with social norms). This is a better way of explaining the complicated differences in political life: for example, two Labour MPs may feel the same way about taxation, but have very different views on terror laws; or two Conservatives may feel very similarly about the importance of the family, but one believes the best way to help is through tax cuts, while the other believes some public spending would be more effective.

One of the most interesting questions I was asked while writing this book was: 'Can you be right wing and altruistic?' Many on the political right want taxes cut so that people can decide how to spend their own money; by the same token, it's perfectly possible to hold the opposite point of view in good faith, and people from all parts of the political spectrum volunteer their spare time altruistically. One of my key assumptions in writing this book is that people can be motivated by good intentions whichever part of the political spectrum they occupy, so I've tried not to take sides on either the left–right or the authoritarian–libertarian spectrum.

Is politics as bad as it seems?

When I was writing this book I came across a great quote from the US politician Adlai Stevenson. He said that a politician is someone who 'approaches every problem with an open mouth'. This slightly sceptical view of the political classes is often twisted – so much so, in fact, that they often appear ignorant, sleazy and only in it for themselves. Whilst it's hard to avoid that description for some, I don't believe it's true for most, and this book has been written with that in mind.

A final thought

This book has been great fun to write. I hope I've got most things about right and that you'll enjoy reading it, but I'm equally hopeful that you'll let me know where I haven't, or you haven't. So either way, please drop me a line at britishpoliticsunravelled@hotmail.co.uk and let me know.

1

The constitution

Does Britain have a constitution?

People often assume that because we don't have a 'written' constitution, we don't have one at all. In fact, since a constitution simply describes how different parts of the state relate to each other – rather like a biology book describing the relationship between the heart and the lungs – it would be hard to function without one.

Where the British constitution differs from those of most other countries is that it is not a single, identifiable document. This does not mean that none of it is 'written' – in fact much of it is (for example laws – see below), but whereas my American friends can point to one slim volume on their bookshelves which contains their constitution, I've got almost a whole bookshelf interpreting ours.

This is mainly because no single event has defined the modern era in Britain (unlike the United States or France, for example, which had their revolutions), and as a result our constitution has developed in fits and starts. Many important parts of the constitution developed to deal with various crises and difficulties, and they often remained unchanged for centuries. Sometimes this was because they worked well, and sometimes because nobody could be bothered to change them: the British constitution is a classic example of the 'if it ain't broke, don't fix it' rule.

So how is the constitution made?

There are several important sources of the constitution, and hence several ways in which it can be changed. The first is by passing laws – any law which defines the relationship between different parts of the state is regarded as part of the constitution. The laws setting up the Scottish Parliament and reforming the House of Lords are therefore part of the constitution.

Because much of this legislation was passed in bits and pieces over the centuries, understanding it is often very complicated. When the government recently wanted to abolish the post of Lord Chancellor, for example, they found almost 1,200 references in hundreds of laws, and they would all need to be changed.

A further source of the constitution is common law, known as 'precedent', which builds up from court decisions. Judges are supposed to follow precedents set in higher courts, so when courts rule on constitutional laws their judgments in turn become part of the constitution.

The third way is through tradition, or 'convention'. These conventions have often built up over many years, and some are incredibly important – often acquiring the force of law (see box). They can be changed, but if a government wants to do so there is sometimes an outcry and it will have to consider if it is worth the trouble.

One convention which has changed in the last twenty years is that Prime Ministers only used to answer questions in the House of Commons about issues for which they were personally responsible. In the 1970s Prime Ministers would never answer questions about the details of hospital management or train strikes, unless they were personally involved. But anyone who has watched Prime Minister's Questions knows that they now answer questions about pretty much anything.

Some important conventions

1. The Queen will sign Bills even if she disagrees with them
2. The Speaker of the House of Commons is politically impartial
3. The Prime Minister should be a member of the House of Commons
4. MPs cannot call each other liars in the House of Commons
5. Ministers must resign if they disagree with a policy once it has been agreed
6. The Queen dissolves Parliament when the Prime Minister asks her to
7. The government will resign if it loses an election or a major vote in Parliament

Authoritative books which include a lot of these conventions are sometimes seen as constitutional texts themselves. One, generally known as 'Erskine May' (after its first author, who wrote it in 1861), sets out all the rules of Parliament. It is the authoritative work on parliamentary procedure and is regarded as a constitutional text.

The final major source is the royal prerogative. In general, this gives ministers the authority to take some decisions without reference to Parliament, and very few prerogatives remain with the Queen personally. Originally, it was the basis of almost all power in the country – the King or Queen had the 'prerogative' to act but since they didn't really govern, ministers instead used the prerogative on their behalf.

Today, the royal prerogative covers some of the most important powers which the government has. They include the power to go to war without consulting the public or even Parliament, signing treaties and conducting diplomacy, and reorganising the civil service.

Has it been changing a lot recently?

It has. There were a lot of changes under Margaret Thatcher in the 1980s, and since 1997 the Labour government has embarked upon a far-reaching programme of constitutional reform. This programme is considered throughout the rest of the book, but to get an idea of the extent of the changes, the box below lists the major ones.

Aside from these laws, two important constitutional 'conventions' have been established:

- The use of referendums to decide contentious issues. There had been only four before 1997, but since then there have been more than thirty. They have decided all sorts of things, from whether Scotland should have its own Parliament to whether Hartlepool should have an elected mayor.

- Judicial review, when courts decide whether new laws are legal or whether government actions comply with laws already passed. This had been underway before 1997 but has sped up since then.

Labour's constitutional reforms
1. The Human Rights Act
2. Setting up the Scottish Parliament, the Welsh Assembly, the Northern Ireland Assembly and the London Assembly
3. Reforms to the House of Lords
4. Introducing proportional representation for many elections across the UK
5. The Freedom of Information Act
6. Independence for the Bank of England
7. Elected mayors in local government
8. Establishing a Supreme Court

The reason this has been possible is that the British constitution is pretty simple to change. Most other countries make it hard to reform their constitutions – they often stipulate that you must have a referendum (when everyone gets to vote on a single issue), or a 60 per cent majority in Parliament, or something similar. In Britain, there is no such barrier – a government simply needs to pass a law. Sometimes this is really controversial; on other occasions it slips by almost unnoticed.

Shouldn't the constitution be brought together in one place?

Many people think it should be. They would like a fully written constitution, like the American one, which would bring all the conventions and all the existing law together in one place and avoid the difficulty of keeping track of all the various bits and pieces. They argue that the more informal arrangements make it too easy for a strong Prime Minister to exercise power with little restraint.

Supporters of the current arrangements point to the remarkable stability that Britain has enjoyed, and argue that our more informal system means the constitution can be changed more easily when it needs to be.

What are the basic principles of the constitution?

There are a few basics which run through everything. The most important of these – 'constitutional monarchy' and 'liberal democracy' – are shorthand for the type of constitution, and country, we have.

Although they sound like something from a school textbook, the ideas are really simple. A constitutional monarchy just means that while its monarch (the Queen) is nominally in charge, in fact the people's representatives are. A liberal democracy means that ordinary people choose governments in free elections, while state interference in their private lives is restricted.

Constitutional laws and conventions regulate the relationships between everything from the monarchy to local and European government, the courts and the public. But there are a few other principles which dictate how the constitution operates – almost like rules for the rules. Several of them have changed dramatically in the last few years.

Unitary state. In Britain, there is only one centre of power – Parliament – and all other parliaments and assemblies are subordinate to it. When the Scottish Parliament was created in 1999, it was because the Westminster Parliament passed a law for it; although it would be pretty unlikely, Westminster could just as easily pass a law to abolish it.

Parliamentary sovereignty. 'Sovereignty' (or supreme authority) lies with Parliament – rather than the monarch, for example, or the people. Two recent developments have left this principle a bit confused. First, British membership of the European Union means that some European law now trumps British law (more on this in Chapter 4). Second, because the royal prerogative allows ministers to take many important decisions without referring to Parliament, some critics of the current arrangements argue that parliamentary sovereignty is incomplete.

Ministerial responsibility. Exactly what it says on the tin: ministers are responsible for everything that happens in their department, whether they did it personally or not. They should defend their departments and not blame their civil servants, and in return the civil servants are supposed to keep quiet if it is the minister's fault. Of course, the ultimate way to take responsibility is to resign, if the cock-up is serious enough. In 1982 the Foreign Secretary, Lord Carrington, resigned when his diplomacy failed and Argentina invaded the Falkland Islands, leading to the Falklands War. Some critics complain that ministers have since become more reluctant to resign. For example, in 1992, when Britain was forced out of the European exchange rate mechanism and British economic policy was turned on its head, and again in 2003, when the government's reasons for going to war in Iraq turned out to have been completely wrong, no minister resigned.

Accountable government. While ministers may not be terribly keen on resigning these days, at least it's obvious when they're responsible. Because of our unitary state, there is a clear line of accountability from the most junior minister right up to the Prime Minister.

Representative government. The public elect MPs, who govern on their behalf. This part of the constitution is often mis-understood to mean that MPs should do what their constituents want; in fact it means almost the opposite – MPs should do what they believe to be right, regardless of what anyone else thinks. Of course, MPs sometimes do this at their peril: when they really buck their voters' wishes, they risk getting booted out of office.

Voters in Bethnal Green and Bow kick out their MP

In the 2005 general election Oona King, a Labour MP, lost her seat to George Galloway, a former Labour MP. The voters of Bethnal Green and Bow kicked out King because she supported the government's war in Iraq. Many of her constituents were Muslims, who opposed the war and were angry that their MP didn't reflect their views on this important issue. King defended her decision vigorously, but lost to anti-war campaigner Galloway. The principle of representative government ran up against the passions and controversy caused by the Iraq war.

Moderate, stable and effective government. Again, exactly what it says on the tin. There have been relatively few radical governments – in general they have been moderate. Unlike in many other countries, British governments have been stable, mostly holding office for full four- or five-year terms. Even when there are divisions within the governing party, governments generally hold together. This is a good record compared to other countries – since 1945, France has had two changes of its constitution and, at the time of writing, Italy has been through some sixty governments! Finally, 'effective government' might seem like an odd one since there are so many complaints about everything from dirty hospitals to late trains. But 'effective government' just means that, unlike other countries, in Britain if the government takes a decision it's likely to get its way. This is because of the unitary state. In other systems, like that of the United States, the government is often frustrated by other people in the political system.

Civil rights. Civil rights – including civil liberties, equality before the law and freedom from discrimination – belong to every citizen. In Britain they come from both statutory law (laws passed in Parliament) and common law (law developed from court decisions). Civil rights were first set out in 1215 in the Magna Carta (which literally means 'great charter'). King John was forced to sign it by the English barons. It recognised the barons' rights, which were later extended to everyone, which is why it's often regarded as the most important document in British constitutional history. It was also the first time such rights had been set out anywhere in the world, and the Magna Carta's principles are the basis for the civil rights laid down in many other countries' written constitutions. Human rights have been dramatically increased by the Human Rights Act (see Chapter 10).

How is this different from America?

The American system is an interesting comparison, because while many of the institutions are the same they are arranged in a different way.

One of the most important differences is in the relationship between the three branches of government common to all political systems:

- Legislature – the parliament, which makes laws
- Executive – the government, which puts laws into practice
- Judiciary – the courts, which uphold the laws.

In the United States (see the box below), these branches are kept separate. In Britain there is a great deal of crossover and while the three branches are equal in theory, in reality the executive is by far the most powerful. The epitome of this crossover is in the role of the Lord Chancellor, who at the time of writing was still a senior member of all three branches (but this is about to change). Some people call this British system an 'elective dictatorship' because it gives a government – even one with a very small majority in Parliament – so much power. Each of these branches of government is considered in a separate chapter.

> **How different it could be – the US model**
> The three branches of government in the United States are described as 'separate but equal', and the system is called 'separation of powers'. In reality they're not totally

separate: one academic called it 'separate institutions sharing powers' – for example, the President appoints judges and their appointments must be approved by Congress, but judges can then rule against both the President and Congress.

What isn't in doubt is that the executive (the President) has far fewer powers. The system works more slowly than in Britain and the President can't expect to get his way all the time.

Making his task even more complicated is the American federal system. This gives the federal government few powers in many areas. Instead the states have a great deal of power over policies such as unemployment benefits, health insurance and education. So the system is much less centralised than in Britain, and more difficult to govern from the centre.

2

Government

'Government' is a bit of a catch-all term, including politicians and ministers in government departments, the departments themselves, and their civil servants. Together they form the executive branch of government, which carries out the laws passed by the legislative branch (Parliament). The government has enormous resources at its disposal to carry out the laws, and immensely complicated procedures to ensure that it does it properly.

Who runs the government?

The complicated answer, and one which prompts lots of further questions, is: lots of people run the government. The short answer is: the Prime Minister is in charge. The gap between the Prime Minister and the next most powerful person in Britain is now larger than ever before. And the situation has changed dramatically even in the last thirty years.

In fact, the British government used to be (and, at least in theory, still is) run by a group of the most senior ministers: the Cabinet. They held debates behind closed doors, reached agreement and then pursued that collective decision. Walter Bagehot, the most famous constitutional analyst, called the Cabinet the 'efficient secret of the English Constitution'.

But Bagehot wrote that in 1867, and today the Prime Minister is no longer *primus inter pares* (first among equals); he runs the government. Government is now like a major company, with the Cabinet as its board. At a weekly meeting its members have occasional discussions on strategy or get a presentation from someone in the marketing or PR department before a big product launch; but in general it is a convenient venue for the chief executive – who really runs it – or the finance officer – who wants to – to announce the week's business.

So how is the government organised?

The government is organised into departments, each covering a general area of responsibility. Each department is headed by a Cabinet minister, assisted by several junior ministers. The senior civil servant in each department is the permanent secretary, who will assist the ministers in carrying out their policies.

The Prime Minister is responsible for making and unmaking departments. And while some have remained reasonably intact for a long time – such as the Treasury – others have been created, dismantled and re-created many times over the years. The departments responsible for trade, industry and energy, for example, went through so many different incarnations between the 1960s and the 1980s that you could write a book about it, and someone probably will. The end result of all this changing is that while some departments have reasonably clear and well-defined responsibilities others have some odd ones which don't seem to fit in their general area.

Departments aren't the only organisations in government, though. In the 1980s the government set up a number of 'executive agencies' and delegated specific responsibilities to them – the Prison Service, for example, became responsible for running prisons, and the much-criticised Child Support Agency is responsible for getting child support money out of absent parents. The aim in setting up the agencies was to allow them to focus more closely on their responsibilities than would a general government department, and they have largely succeeded.

A third type of organisation is a quango (see box below), and the final type is a task force. Task forces have been a particular favourite of the Labour government – it has set up hundreds. They are set up to bring experts together to consider a specific issue, and are then supposed to be disbanded. But critics complain that they are really designed to kick tough political issues into the long grass, and then allow the government to evade responsibilty for controversial solutions proposed by the task force.

What is a quango?

'Quango' stands for 'quasi-autonomous non-governmental organisation' and means a body which is operationally independent but relies on government funding – for example Arts Council England or the Commission for Racial Equality. Some people are very critical of quangos because they spend a lot of public money but are much less answerable to parliament for it than a government department would be.

Why are modern Prime Ministers so powerful?

Prime Ministers are a funny breed. On a day-to-day basis, their formal powers are rather limited while their powers to influence are very substantial indeed.

Most ministers get their power from being head of a government department. The Chancellor of the Exchequer runs the

Treasury and can issue new rules about tax collection, for example, and the minister for planning can change the planning rules. On a day-to-day basis, they make hundreds of decisions which affect people's lives. The Prime Minister is different: most of his powers (see box below) come either from convention, or from the royal prerogative – powers which the PM and government formally wield in the name of the monarch, but which in reality the monarch has no control over.

The Prime Minister's formal powers

1. Declaring war
2. Use of nuclear weapons
3. Appointing and dismissing ministers
4. Chairing the Cabinet and its most important committees
5. Calling an election and dissolving Parliament
6. Appointing bishops, peers, senior civil servants, diplomats, judges, European Commissioners and chairs of public bodies
7. Setting up and abolishing government departments
8. Controlling the civil service
9. Interpreting the constitution
10. Giving honours
11. Relations with other heads of government, attending summits, signing and ratifying treaties
12. Managing the government's relationship with the monarch
13. Managing the government's relationship with the opposition
14. Ultimate oversight of the secret services
15. Overall responsibility for the government's media strategy

This growth in prime ministerial powers in relation to other politicians is associated with two trends:

- improved discipline within parties, which has given Prime Ministers (and other party leaders) more *power* within the political system;
- personalisation within the media, which emphasises the role of party leaders, and gives the Prime Minister in particular greater *influence* within the system, for example by setting the political and media agenda.

These general trends have been exacerbated by the command-and-control tendencies of two recent Prime Ministers, Margaret Thatcher and Tony Blair.

Is the Prime Minister now more like a president?

Prime Ministers are in many ways *more* powerful than American Presidents. The most important reason is a Prime Minister's more secure position in Parliament, which means they can be sure of getting their legislative programme passed. The US system has far more 'checks and balances'. So Presidents often find themselves bargaining with politicians from other parties just to get some basic co-operation in Congress.

However there is one important respect in which PMs are weaker. Because they aren't directly elected by the people, when their party decides it has had enough, they don't need to wait for an election to boot them out.

In addition, the President is both head of government (like the Prime Minister) and head of state (like the Queen) and Commander-in-Chief of the US armed forces. This means that his ceremonial role is much greater than the Prime Minister's.

So what goes on in No. 10?

No. 10 Downing Street is the Prime Minister's official residence (see box below). In the late 1950s the Prime Minister, Harold Macmillan, was nicknamed 'Supermac' because he was seen as so powerful. But it didn't look like that to him because he had very little staff support in No. 10. As prime ministerial responsibilities have grown over the last fifty years, successive Prime Ministers have gradually built up their office. They have increased the number of staff and the variety of functions, and it is now a substantial institution.

Why No. 10?

No. 10 has been the official home of the Prime Minister since King George II gave it to Sir Robert Walpole in the 1730s. Walpole was the first 'prime minister', but the phrase was coined as an insult to Walpole's grandeur: his official title was First Lord of the Treasury. That remains one of the Prime Minister's titles today, and it is still written on the letterbox of No. 10.

Behind the famous black door is a maze of offices from which the PM directs the business of government. But No. 10 is actually two buildings merged together – the smaller house on Downing Street and a much grander building just behind, on Horse Guards Parade. It is far larger than it looks from the outside, and houses both the Prime Minister's office and his home, a small flat at the top (although when Labour came to power in 1997 Tony Blair, married and then with three children, swapped this with the Chancellor, Gordon Brown, who was single at the time, for the larger flat above Nos. 11 and 12).

The two other buildings in Downing Street are also owned by the government. No. 11 is home to the Chancellor, and No. 12 was the Chief Whip's office until very recently – it is now home to the Prime Minister's press office.

Recent Prime Ministers have found two units in No. 10 particularly useful:

- The Policy Directorate (previously the Policy Unit) helps the PM develop new policies and co-ordinate them across government. Until it was created in 1974 almost all the government's policy development happened in individual departments.
- The Press Office communicates to the public what the PM and government are trying to do. It is extremely busy, dealing with hundreds of requests every day.

Both these offices contain a mixture of civil servants and politically appointed 'special advisers'. Politicians generally bring in special advisers to help them decide and communicate the more party political aspects of their job, although some are policy specialists – such as academics – brought in from outside the government.

Although special advisers and civil servants work together, their jobs are often very different. In particular, civil servants are not meant to do party political work (attacking the other parties or planning the government's next manifesto, for example). Some critics have criticised the Labour government for blurring this boundary. They cite the two special advisers – Alastair Campbell and Jonathan Powell, respectively the former Downing Street director of communications and the current chief of staff – who were given special powers so they could give instructions to civil servants. More recently the government was criticised for redefining the role of special advisers to 'assist' ministers rather than merely 'advising' them.

Other critics complain that this growth of political appointees is making the British Prime Minister too presidential, but although the number of staff has grown enormously the office is still far smaller than the offices of the US President or even the Australian Prime Minister.

Still, some observers looking at all the bodies created by Tony Blair, and the way he has fused the functions of No. 10 with those of the Cabinet Office, argue that the two are effectively a Prime Minister's Department.

Which 'insiders' really advise the Prime Minister?

The amazing thing about the PM's advisers is how often they change. They usually come from four groups:

1. Other ministers, who are both experienced politicians and responsible for taking most government decisions, so Prime Ministers would do well to listen to their advice. Despite this, though, few PMs are really close to more than a handful of their ministerial colleagues.

2. Civil servants, who are constitutionally responsible for advising the PM. Usually, a few of the many officials in Downing Street become close to the PM (see 'Is it like *Yes, Minister?*' below).

3. Special advisers. The press love to hate them, but there are lots of these politically appointed advisers in Downing Street. Because they can speak to the PM more easily than most other people who want to, they're often assumed to be very influential. Some are – because they work for the PM and not the government as a whole, they are more devoted and hence more loyal – but most aren't as influential as they'd like to think.

4. Informal advisers. Many Prime Ministers want to hear as many different perspectives as possible, and have a wide variety of informal advisers. They can be everything from political allies, journalists and businessmen to their spouse and old schoolfriends.

Very few advisers are influential on every subject. And of course Prime Ministers often have their own views and ignore the advice altogether!

How do they co-ordinate the rest of government?

One of the main changes to government since Labour came to power in 1997 has been the development of a 'co-ordination' role in No. 10 and the Cabinet Office. Before then, for example, there was no systematic way of checking what departments were getting up to and often no systematic way of ensuring they worked in a co-ordinated fashion and delivered what was expected of them. New Labour ministers regarded this as a particular problem for issues affecting more than one government department (see the drugs example below).

'Joined-up government': drug policy

The annoying phrase 'joined-up government' was coined to emphasise the need for departments to work together to solve problems, rather than fight with each other.

Drug abuse is a good example of a problem in which numerous government departments and agencies have an interest, and why a special unit was set up in the Cabinet Office to co-ordinate policy. All these departments have an interest in drugs policy, which explains why it's so hard to co-ordinate without a special unit:

- the Home Office (for the police and probation services)
- the Department of Constitutional Affairs (for the courts)
- the Department of Health (for the NHS)
- the Department for Education and Skills (for education about the dangers)
- the Foreign Office (to negotiate with drug-producing countries)
- the Treasury (for Revenue & Customs)

Is someone keeping tabs on whether they're actually delivering?

The Labour government since 1997 has introduced two important mechanisms for monitoring the performance of government departments, and making sure they 'deliver':

- the 'public service agreements' (or PSAs) which the Treasury makes with each department. These set out what the department will do with the cash it's given by the Treasury;
- the monitoring mechanisms in the Cabinet Office. Several new units have sprung up, but the most important is the Delivery Unit, which sounds like it should be in a hospital and not monitoring them. It monitors the targets the government has set itself, ensures that departments are on track for meeting them, and suggests remedies if they appear to be off track. This is a genuine innovation in British government but its success (and survival under a future government) is by no means certain.

What is a 'spin doctor'?

A spin doctor is a press officer or political adviser whose job is to persuade the media – and through them the public – to accept their interpretation (or 'spin') of a story.

Recently they have been getting a very bad reputation: many people worry that 'spinning' is little more than lying. Critics of 'spin' say the public must be able to trust the facts they receive from their politicians, even if they don't always agree with their interpretation. They worry that this type of media manipulation undermines public trust in the government and in politics generally.

In reality, while they do sometimes try to obscure the facts, more often than not spin doctors just try to persuade journalists to concentrate on a part of the story which is more favourable to them. Many spin doctors, and others who work in politics, also argue that journalists themselves are sometimes guilty of spinning to make stories more interesting.

If the Prime Minister is so powerful, what does the Cabinet do?

The Cabinet is the group of the government's most senior ministers. Getting into the Cabinet is what most MPs and junior ministers aspire to do. It varies in size but at present comprises the Prime Minister and Deputy Prime Minister, fourteen secretaries of state and seven other senior ministers.

For much of the last century, the Cabinet was where most key political decisions were taken. It began as a committee of the Privy Council – the group which used to advise the monarch – and before politicians join the Cabinet they still have to become Privy Counsellors (allowing them to be known as 'Right Honourable' in the House of Commons, rather than just 'Honourable').

But key political decisions are increasingly taken by the Prime Minister. The way Prime Ministers use their Cabinets has changed, although it varies from one PM to another depending on how useful they think it is. Some use it a lot; others, like Tony Blair, bypass it in favour of a less formal style of government – with 'chats' between senior ministers – which some critics have dubbed 'the sofa Cabinet'.

How the Cabinet can get ignored – the Millennium Dome

Sometimes, even when Cabinet ministers have discussed things, their views are completely ignored. In his 2001 documentary *Cabinet Confidential*, journalist Michael Cockerell reported the inside story of how the Millennium Dome was approved.

Cockerell reported that following a Cabinet discussion where most ministers were against the Dome, those views were reported to Tony Blair by his deputy, John Prescott. Within two hours of the Cabinet meeting ending Blair announced that the project would go ahead.

'But', Cockerell suggested to Prescott, 'the Cabinet itself hadn't taken that decision to go ahead with the Dome.'

Prescott replied, 'Well, in the sense that when the Cabinet makes a decision, what we don't have is a vote on it. There's never been a vote. There's these mysterious areas of Cabinet, you take soundings and voices. And I gave him the voice, and I gave him what I thought the best possible position was, and which would accommodate most of those views of the Cabinet, and he made a decision based on that. I didn't hear of any resignations afterwards, did you?'

So is the Cabinet still important?

It's still a club most politicians want to belong to, so in that sense it is important. However, most observers are now more interested in the 'Cabinet system' rather than the weekly meetings of just the Cabinet itself. The Cabinet system includes Cabinet sub-committees and the Cabinet Office (which takes and circulates minutes and so on).

But since 2004, the government has begun to move away from the sofa Cabinet and back towards more formal arrangements, with formal Cabinet committees instead of chats. Its advocates say this system allows decisions to be properly discussed and recorded, and makes it easier for the people who need to implement the decisions – mainly the civil servants – to know what they're supposed to be implementing.

In the privy

The Privy Council, one of the oldest parts of the government, was once the monarch's advisory committee. The Cabinet was originally one of its sub-committees, which is why when Cabinet ministers are appointed they still have to become members of the Privy Council. Appointments to the Council are for life, though, so its more than 500 members are allowed to call themselves 'Right Honourable'.

The Council meets about once a month, although its only real business is for the Queen to formally approve 'Orders in Council' – decisions taken by the government in her name. Only current members of the government attend these meetings.

The other use of the Privy Council is to brief senior members of the opposition parties on sensitive issues. When this happens, it is often on 'Privy Council terms', so called because of the oath members take when they join the council: to 'keep secret all matters . . . treated of in Council'.

How do Ministers get appointed?

The Prime Minister has to appoint about 115 ministers, junior and senior, in the government. They must belong to one of the Houses of Parliament because they are responsible to it, but can be either an MP or a member of the House of Lords (known as peers). However, there is a convention that relatively few Cabinet ministers are peers, and there is rarely more than one other peer per department.

The Prime Minister must balance a number of factors when appointing ministers, not just whether they will be good at the job. For example, political parties contain people with lots of different views and Prime Ministers usually want to appoint a variety of people from across the party. However, those who are loyal or politically sympathetic to the Prime Minister will usually find themselves in more important positions. In the early 1980s, when few other government ministers were sympathetic to her economic views, Margaret Thatcher made sure she put those who were in all the key economic departments. And trouble-makers will often find themselves appointed junior ministers – a job that can stop them criticising the government in public but without giving them the room to cause trouble inside the government.

In addition, Prime Ministers usually want to ensure that the government fairly reflects the diversity of the country. For example, quite apart from their ability most Prime Ministers want to ensure there is a good spread of MPs from different parts of the country, as well as appointing women and people from ethnic minorities as ministers.

Waiting to see what job it is . . .

When a government reshuffle is under way, ambitious MPs often wait nervously by the phone for a call from No. 10 – either for the offer of a job, or for a request to come and see the Prime Minister in person. This section is from the memoirs of Edwina Currie, describing the moment she was first appointed a minister in the 1980s.

'Now it would not do to run along Whitehall, either – I had to retain some vestige of dignity. So even if it meant I was going to be a few minutes late, I was going to walk, steadily. There were not going to be any photographs of me looking scatty in the following day's newspapers; I would make sure of that. And so I nodded to the policemen, who smiled knowingly, swept past the pressmen, and strolled up to the door.

'It opened as I arrived and there she was, smart in blue, of course. "Ah! Edwina. I'm glad you've arrived. Now we can get on." And then the offer – the Department of Health, the one I had hoped I might get, after years of working in the Health Service.

'Another door opened and we came into one of the drawing-rooms, chandeliers now twinkling as the lights were turned on and staff brought drinks in huge tumblers. The door into government had opened wide for several of us. There were half a dozen of my colleagues, some erstwhile back-benchers like myself, others taken from the Whip's Office, all in a slight faze and unsure of the etiquette for a moment like this.'

From *Life Lines: Politics and Health 1986–1988* (London: Sidgwick & Jackson, 1989), page 3.

Is there a career ladder?

Certainly. Many ministers start their days as a parliamentary private secretary (PPS), an unpaid bag-carrier to a more senior minister. A PPS is considered part of the government and is expected to remain totally loyal. Being appointed a PPS is a sign that they might get a 'proper job' in the next reshuffle.

Next come the whips and the junior ministers. These jobs carry additional salaries on top of the standard MP's salary. The whips are the government business managers in Parliament –

making sure MPs and peers vote the way they are supposed to. Junior ministers are usually called parliamentary under-secretaries of state.

The next step is to be a minister of state. This probably won't be in the same department as previously. Ministers normally shift around quite a bit between different departments: the theory is that they don't need to be policy experts, because that is the job of the civil servants. A minister of state is the most senior minister outside the Cabinet.

The Cabinet is the top of what the former PM Benjamin Disraeli called the political 'greasy pole'. More importantly, Cabinet ministers usually have their own departments to run, which gives them a wide range of powers. Yet even within the Cabinet there is a hierarchy, with the three most senior departments being the Treasury, the Foreign Office and the Home Office.

What happens at the end?

The end of a political career can come extremely suddenly. Usually, it is pretty unwelcome. Yet sacking their colleagues (or being a 'good butcher') is a skill Prime Ministers have to learn. Margaret Thatcher once said, 'I'm not a good butcher but I've had to learn to carve the joint,' while Tony Blair is regarded as bad at it.

Labour Prime Minister Clement Attlee was famous for his economy with words, but one of his colleagues was horrified when, having asked why he had been sacked, Attlee replied simply, 'Not up to it.'

These butchery skills are associated with another word in the political lexicon – the 'reshuffle'. Ministers on the up look forward to reshuffles for promotion, whereas those at the top often find themselves looking over their shoulders.

In Britain, reshuffles mean that ministers tend not to stay in their jobs very long – often for shorter periods than in many other countries. Since it takes a long time for a minister to become an expert on an area of policy, many observers think it's odd to move them once they have. While few people think it's a good system, most politicians accept that the need for a government to appear 'fresh' and 'dynamic' usually comes first.

And how much do they get paid?

Ministers are paid a salary on top of their pay as an MP. At 2006 rates, an MP's basic salary is £59,000; whips receive an extra £25,000, parliamentary under-secretaries an extra £29,000, ministers of state an extra £39,000 and Cabinet ministers receive £75,000. The Prime Minister is paid £125,000 on top of his parliamentary salary, giving a total of £184,000.

Because members of the House of Lords don't receive an annual salary (they get paid a daily allowance of £75 instead), their ministerial salary is higher than for MPs, but the combined total is much less. Strangely, all these government salaries are quite a bit less than what the top civil servants get paid.

Why do ministers all agree, even when we know they disagree?

Because of what is probably the most important doctrine in government – collective responsibility. It comes from the days when the Cabinet took all the decisions. The theory went like this: ministers with a variety of views on an issue would debate it thoroughly and agree a decision collectively. Once they had done so, they either had to accept the decision or resign from the

Cabinet. If they didn't, the decision wouldn't be collective and the government would be in disarray. As one Victorian Prime Minister, Lord Melbourne, once told his Cabinet, 'it doesn't matter what you decide, so long as you all tell the same story'.

Many things have changed about this doctrine since then, not least the fact that agreements are rarely reached collectively. But the rule that ministers must defend government decisions or resign, even when they disagree with them, has remained. One well-known example of defending a government decision involved the former Conservative minister, Chris Patten: in the 1980s he was responsible for legislation introducing the poll tax, even though he disagreed with it privately.

Where do civil servants fit in?

Civil servants are the officials who work in government departments. They are strictly non-political – civil servants have to serve whichever political party is in power. So they stay in their jobs when the government changes. This also means that they can spend their whole career working in government, often in many different departments.

There are two types of civil servant. Most work in administrative grades – actually putting into effect the policies of the government. The top tiers, though, also have policy-making roles. They advise ministers on which policies the government should adopt, and are sometimes known as 'mandarins'.

Is it really like *Yes, Minister*?
The relationship between civil servants and their ministers was satirised in the TV series *Yes, Minister* and *Yes, Prime Minister*, which had an extraordinary effect on the way British people thought about the civil service.

The series revolved around the relationship between an ambitious but rather clueless minister, Jim Hacker, and his permanent secretary (the title given to the most senior civil servant in a department), Sir Humphrey Appleby. Each episode was a duel between the two, but the underlying theme was that the civil servants thought they knew best, and they really ran the government.

Great satire works best when it exaggerates reality, and the same is certainly true of *Yes, Minister*. Because civil servants are like the 'permanent staff', they do see policies in a longer timeframe, and they may not always share the political inclinations of their ministers. They may sometimes think they know better. But in general, they are devoted to their vocation and determined to serve the government of the day. The programme, though, helped influence the views of a generation of ministers, in many cases leading them to treat their civil servants more cautiously.

Who is in charge of the civil service?

The head of the civil service is called the Cabinet Secretary. He is like a chief operating officer for the civil service as it tries to implement the government's policies, as well as being the Prime Minister's senior adviser. The various units and directorates in the Cabinet Office report to the PM through the Cabinet Secretary.

The Cabinet Secretary is also in charge of civil service reform, which has become one of the organisation's most urgent priorities in recent years. It includes

- attracting people from more diverse backgrounds;
- improving its 'delivery' of public services (such as education and healthcare);

- enhancing its professional skills – the civil service has historically been full of generalists and is now looking for more specialists;
- moving offices out of London into the regions;
- reducing staff numbers.

Why is it called 'Whitehall'?

The whole system of government departments is known collectively as Whitehall because that is the name of the road in central London where most of them are based. It is a great wide road, running from Trafalgar Square towards Parliament Square, and most of the important departments have their headquarters on it. Whitehall is in Westminster, in central London, which itself provides the name used to describe the entire national political system – government, parliament, political parties – based there.

Does everything happen in Westminster?

No. A lot of governing goes on away from Westminster – at either a local or an international level. In recent years those levels – particularly the European – have become increasingly important. The role they play is considered in later chapters.

3

Elections

Elections are a crucial part of how British democracy works. They facilitate one of the core theories underlying the British constitution – liberal, or representative, democracy.

The British don't quite have the American appetite for electing public officials – in some American states voters have to elect people to fill almost fifty offices, everything from the local dog collector to the President of the United States. Nevertheless, British elections are regular, and vigorous, exercises in democracy. In recent years there have been two important developments in the way they operate:

- the introduction of new voting systems, with proportional representation (PR) introduced for the first time in regional and European elections;
- increasing worries about turnout. In one by-election in 1999, fewer than one in five voters bothered to cast their ballot, and turnout in recent general elections has been well down on what it once was.

The rest of this chapter explains how elections work, why they sometimes don't, and what impact these and other changes are having. We'll start with the most important elections.

How is the House of Commons elected?

As of 2006 the House of Commons comprises 646 members of Parliament (MPs), each elected in an electoral district or constituency. For these elections we use a system known as 'First Past the Post' (FPTP). In each constituency, the candidate who wins the most votes is elected MP.

Voters cast their vote for an individual candidate, yet in reality most voters are actually voting for the candidate's party, and often know very little about the individual. However, many MPs do take their responsibilities to their constituents seriously, and most people involved in politics believe the constituency link is important – keeping MPs in touch with people's problems and knowing what needs to change.

This same system is also used in local elections in England, Scotland and Wales (although there are plans to change it in Scotland). Local elections in Northern Ireland use a form of PR.

Are all votes equal?

In theory, yes. But one criticism of FPTP is that it makes some people's votes more valuable than others. In parts of the country where there is a strong feeling towards a particular party, constituencies become 'safe' – no other party realistically expects to win them. For example all the seats in Glasgow are safe for Labour, and many seats in Sussex are similarly safe for the Conservatives.

This means that the parties can rely on those seats, and don't spend much time, money or effort campaigning there. Instead, they concentrate on parts of the country where they are worried they might lose seats, or hope they can gain them: these are known as 'marginal' constituencies. Yet even there, most parties have a certain core of supporters who will always vote for them, and won't switch to another party. This leaves a very small number of voters who might move between parties – so-called 'swing' voters. Only quite small numbers of swing voters need change parties to have a very large impact on the election result. In fact, so disproportionate is their influence that, in 2005, if just 13,501 people had voted differently Labour's 66-seat House of Commons majority would have been reduced to zero!

During election campaigns political parties use most of their resources to appeal to swing voters. Even outside elections, the parties often seem more interested in swing voters than the rest of the country and adjust their policies accordingly, hence the criticism that some votes are more highly valued than others.

Is the system fair?

Not really – in addition to making some votes more valuable than others, the constituency-based FPTP system can even allow a government to be formed with fewer votes than the opposition. This happened in 1951 and, more recently, in February 1974.

That, however, is not the whole story. Defenders of FPTP argue that giving a government a proper majority helps it to govern effectively, and means it can sometimes take tough decisions. They say introducing any of the proposed alternatives would mean a series of coalition governments, which would be less stable and less effective. Some forms of voting reform are unpopular because they would remove the constituency link between voters and their elected representatives.

The Liberal Democrats are the party most associated with voting reform. They would certainly be the biggest beneficiary –

at present they usually win about 20 per cent of the vote but only get 10 per cent of MPs. Yet opponents of their preferred alternative, PR, argue that it would result in a series of coalition governments in which the Liberal Democrats were always involved – and that would be just as unfair!

So should we have PR instead?

Most proposed reforms include some element of proportional representation, meaning that a party's **representation** (i.e. MPs, MEPs or councillors) is allocated on the basis of the **proportion** of the votes it receives. Proponents of PR say that this would get away from the biggest problems with the current system, namely:

- individual candidates can win with a small share of the vote in their constituency (less than a third for three MPs in 2005);
- larger parties often end up with far more MPs than their proportion of the votes would deserve, while smaller parties get fewer;
- parties concentrate on swing voters in marginal constituencies and ignore everyone else.

Since 1997 three different types of PR have been introduced: one for elections in Scotland, Wales and London; another for the European Parliament; and a third for the Northern Ireland Assembly. But introducing PR for elections to the House of Commons is still very controversial.

How do these different types of PR work?

Elections to the Scottish Parliament are held under the 'additional member' system, in which people have two votes. One is for their constituency MSP, and 73 of the 129 MSPs are elected in this way under traditional FPTP. The second vote is cast for a political party, and this second vote elects the rest of the MSPs. The aim is for the Parliament to be roughly proportional without entirely losing the link between MSPs and their constituency. What normally happens is this:

- If a party performs well and wins lots of constituency seats, it will get few top-up seats.
- If a party wins few constituency seats (or none at all) but still gets a good number of votes, some of the candidates on its party list will become MSPs. In the most recent elections MSPs were elected for the Green Party, the Scottish Socialist Party and the Scottish Senior Citizens' Unity Party like this.

This system is also used for elections to the Welsh Assembly and the London Assembly. In Wales, 40 of the 60 Assembly members are elected from constituencies, while for London the figures are 14 out of 25.

The 'party list' system, used for elections to the European Parliament, is much simpler. Voters in each region have a single vote, which they cast for a party, rather than a person. MEPs are elected from each party's list according to the proportion of the votes each party receives. This means MEPs no longer have their own constituencies – instead they share responsibility for whole regions.

The system for elections to the Northern Ireland Assembly – the 'single transferable vote' or STV – is the most complicated of the lot, and is dealt with in the box below.

STV in Northern Ireland

Each constituency elects six members of the Legislative Assembly (MLAs), instead of just one, so parties normally put up six candidates per constituency. Voters then rate the candidates in order of preference.

Votes are normally counted in a number of different rounds, and a quota is set (the number of votes cast divided by six). In the first round, any candidate who gets over the quota is elected. After that, votes are transferred away from comfortably elected candidates (their surplus) and from those who did extremely badly and are eliminated, until all six MLAs are elected.

In Northern Ireland, this STV system is also used for elections to the European Parliament *and* in local elections.

What impact does PR have?

The biggest impact is that single parties rarely get a majority of votes – and therefore they equally rarely get a majority of seats. This means parties have to govern in coalitions, as Labour and the Liberal Democrats have done in Scotland since 1999.

However, PR has another important effect: getting rid of 'tactical voting'. Tactical voting describes when a voter backs a party he or she doesn't really support to stop someone they really dislike getting in. For example, in a seat where the battle is between Labour and the Conservatives, a Green Party supporter might vote Labour to stop the Conservatives winning, while a UKIP supporter might back the Conservatives to stop Labour getting in. This effect was particularly pronounced in 1997, to the disadvantage of the Conservatives.

PR encourages people to vote for the party whose policies they most agree with, and smaller parties' share of the vote often increases. For example, the Green Party doubled its share of the vote between the 1994 European elections, which were held under FPTP, and the 1999 elections, which were held under PR. As a result they gained two MEPs, whereas before they had none.

What would be the consequences of a hung Parliament?

When no party has a clear majority in Parliament, it is known as a 'hung Parliament'. Although this does sometimes happen under the current FPTP system, as for example in the February 1974 general election, hung Parliaments are more often associated with PR. In Britain one party hardly ever gets more than 50 per cent of the vote and so wouldn't get a majority under PR.

Under the current arrangements, the party with the largest number of seats might try to make a short-term pact with another, smaller party – for example Labour with the Liberal Democrats – before calling another election to try and get an outright majority. This happened in 1974, when there were two elections in one year. Under PR, parties would have to form longer-lasting coalition governments.

Supporters of PR argue that this would be a good thing. They say the parties in the coalition would be forced to compromise with one another, which would much more accurately reflect what the voters actually wanted – rather than one party getting its way on everything, as at present. They also say that because the parties in the coalition would command the support of more than 50 per cent of the voters, it would have more authority.

Opponents strongly disagree. Their real concerns are with stability and strength of purpose. They say coalition governments are riven with disagreements, and the resulting indecision makes it difficult for them to act firmly to solve the country's problems.

How are British elections organised?

Different types of election are run differently, but all have two things in common. For one, we always vote on Thursdays – it's just a British tradition (in the same way as the Americans run theirs on a Tuesday). Even when we have the European elections, and the counting can't start until Sunday, when everyone across Europe has finished voting, we vote on a Thursday. Second, all elections are run by local councils – they keep the registers of who's eligible to vote, check the candidates' credentials, print the ballot papers, run the polling stations and count the votes.

Elections for everything other than the House of Commons happen on a strict timetable set down in legislation – every four years for local and regional elections, every five years for elections to the European Parliament. Elections to the House of Commons must happen *at least* every five years, but are otherwise at the Prime Minister's discretion.

Why do people sit outside polling stations asking for my card number? Should I tell them anything?

They are known as 'tellers', and are members of the political parties. They take voters' polling numbers so that they know who has voted. The parties then compare this list against their own list of supporters, and then chase up their own people to make sure they vote.

There are strict rules about what tellers and other party supporters are allowed to do near a polling station. They're not allowed to ask you anything on the way in, and they're not allowed to try and persuade you how to vote. You're under no obligation to tell them anything if you don't want to. In very close elections there's sometimes a bit of rivalry between tellers, but more often they have a chat and get on quite well. After all, if you're spending several hours sitting together outside a polling station, there's very little else to do!

Can we trust the results?

Yes. The officials responsible for elections have to be completely impartial – an important difference from the United States, for example, where elected politicians are often responsible for interpreting election rules (as in Florida in the 2000 presidential election).

That is not to say there is never fraud. In the 2005 general election, for example, there were widespread concerns because of some cases of fraud with postal votes in recent local elections. But laws against electoral fraud are tight and the penalties severe. More importantly our political culture is extremely intolerant of fraud, all of which reduces the likelihood of its occurrence.

If postal voting makes fraud easier, why do it?

There have been lots of experiments in recent years with the time, place and manner in which people vote. The aim has been to see if voting can be made quicker and more convenient, and if more people can be encouraged to do it – raising turnout.

The experiments have involved electronic voting (on machines rather than on paper), voting on different days of the week, polling stations in supermarkets, and all-postal voting. The only one of these which really pushed up turnout was all-postal voting, which is why the government has been keen to use it more widely.

Why does turnout matter so much?

Because of what lower turnout implies: that the public is apathetic and isn't engaged with the political process. In a representative democracy like ours, that reduces politicians' legitimacy and makes it harder for winning parties to claim a mandate for government. It ultimately corrodes trust in politicians and the political process.

Politicians of all parties have been getting very worried about the trend of declining turnout in general elections. Although it doesn't fall every time (it rose quite sharply in 1992 compared to 1987, for example, and also rose in 2005 compared to 2001), it is on a downward trend: in 2005 the turnout was just 61.3 per cent, whereas in 1950 it had been 84.1 per cent. There are all sorts of other variations – turnout is higher in Scotland and Northern Ireland, for example, than elsewhere in the UK – and other elections see much lower turnout than the general election.

The trouble is, no one really knows why turnout is falling. There are all sorts of theories – people are bored with politics, they're happy with the direction the country's going, they don't think their vote will change anything because all the parties offer the same thing, they think the result is a foregone conclusion, they don't feel any sense of engagement with politics (this is thought to be especially true among young people), even that it's too hard to vote (hence the experiments to make it easier). Some have even suggested we should introduce compulsory voting – in Australia it increases turnout to around 90 per cent – as a way of dealing with the problem. Others complain that in a liberal democracy people have a right not to vote just as they have a right to vote.

In truth, all these theories probably explain some of the falling turnout. So next time there's a really competitive election with parties offering very different policies on some big issues which everyone is concerned about, turnout will probably rise pretty dramatically, but no one really knows!

Who should I vote for?

For elections held under FPTP, you need to think about four things:

- what matters to you – which issues and which side of those issues you're on;
- which party most closely matches what matters to you – although bear in mind no party will do everything you want it to;
- the views of the candidates in your constituency – you are electing an individual, not just a party, and sometimes individuals from a party you hadn't considered might more closely represent your views;
- the electoral shape of your constituency – if the party you most want to win is very unlikely to win, you might want to vote tactically; that is, for the party closest to your views with a realistic chance of winning. But bear in mind that voting tactically does deprive the party you really support of valuable votes, and amazing results do happen, sometimes.

For elections held under different electoral systems (particularly PR) the role of the individual candidate and constituency politics is much less important. But otherwise the balance between these four will depend on each voter. Some will weigh the MP's personality quite heavily, others will never vote for one party or another no matter how impressive its candidate. Whatever you decide, you'll need to do it on the basis of good information, so getting hold of an informative, non-partisan guide is vital.

Most newspapers publish a guide near election time, although bear in mind that they often approach the election with a slant of their own. The BBC and other broadcasters, who are required to be less partisan, have good websites with issue guides on them. These will also give some figures about previous elections in your constituency.

For finding out about your local candidates, nothing's better than hearing them in person, and local churches usually get together and arrange at least one 'hustings' during the campaign. If you're pressed for time, local newspapers usually have a Q&A section for all the candidates in the run-up to polling day, or you could just call the local party offices – there are always numbers on the back of the leaflets. Very few people call the offices, so it can often be a good way of getting some quick answers. If you get a sudden urge to find discover more when the offices are closed, the parties' websites are always worth a look.

4

Parliament

When most people think of politics, their minds turn either to ministers or to MPs. Parliament is the legislative branch of British governance – that is, it provides the laws which the executive (government) administers and on which the judiciary (the courts) judge. It has two houses – the House of Commons and House of Lords – known together as the Houses of Parliament, or just Parliament. In recent decades governments with large majorities have paid steadily less attention to Parliament, but it still retains a central place in the British political system.

Bills and Acts

A Bill is a piece of legislation being considered by Parliament. Once it is passed, and the Queen has signed it into law, it becomes an Act of Parliament.

What's the difference between the Commons and the Lords?

There are a number of important differences, but perhaps the most important is their role. The House of Commons is the primary chamber, while the House of Lords is a 'revising' chamber. This means that major policy decisions will normally be taken in the House of Commons, while the House of Lords

43

can improve the details of the legislation without challenging its essence.

This principle is part of the 'Salisbury convention', which says that the Lords should not block government legislation contained in a party manifesto. Since the reforms of recent years have increased the legitimacy of the Lords, though, this convention is under pressure, and some more substantial pieces of government business now get challenged.

There are two other important differences:

- Powers: the House of Lords has fewer powers than the Commons – it can only delay legislation for a year, not block it entirely. If it blocks the same Bill two years in a row, the Speaker of the House of Commons can invoke the Parliament Act and pass the Bill anyway.
- Composition: – members of the House of Commons (MPs) are elected, while members of the House of Lords (sometimes known as peers) either inherit the right to sit, or are appointed there for life.

What do MPs do?

MPs are representatives of the people – sent to Parliament to take decisions on our behalf. This is a basic constitutional principle: MPs should do what they believe to be right, regardless of what anyone else thinks. The classic exposition of this argument was by Edmund Burke, who in 1774 told his voters in Bristol: 'Your representative owes you, not his industry only, but his judgment; and he betrays, instead of serving you, if he sacrifices it to your opinion.'

They are elected to legislate, and the government is chosen from amongst MPs and peers. Ministers and party spokesmen in the other parties (collectively known as 'frontbenchers' because they sit on the front benches in Parliament) spend much of their time attending to policy matters. The rest of the MPs, the backbenchers, have an important role too. They are supposed to scrutinise the government – to ensure that its policies are well conceived and effectively implemented, that it is well administered and public money well spent.

There are a number of different parliamentary activities that most MPs take some part in, which are supposed to accomplish all these functions:

- speaking in debates, either on specific pieces of legislation or debates about more general issues, and voting on them;
- asking questions of ministers at Question Time sessions or via written questions;
- sitting on various committees, either to look at specific Bills or to keep an eye on activity within a department (see below);
- suggesting legislation and tabling motions;
- writing to ministers.

Most MPs also spend a great deal of their time helping constituents with all manner of problems which are political but not strictly parliamentary – see the box below.

What could your MP do for you?

Most MPs are happy to help their constituents – you – with all manner of things. Indeed many MPs, who don't get a chance to change government policy or be a minister themselves, say helping individuals is the most satisfying part of the job.

If you are concerned about something to do with government policy, your MP has a range of things he or she could do to raise it on your behalf, such as asking parliamentary questions, writing to the appropriate minister or seeking a debate on the matter in the House of

Commons. All these are excellent ways of getting notice for something you're concerned about.

But it's often when a constituent needs help with a more personal problem that MPs are at their best. If someone has problems with benefits, child support, housing, immigration – any number of social policies – MPs are often very willing to help. What's more, many MPs have researchers with a lot of experience in dealing with the relevant organisations (many of which themselves have special units to deal with requests from MPs), so if your MP takes up your case it may well get dealt with more quickly.

How can you ask for help?

Most MPs have weekly 'surgeries' where constituents can go and see them to discuss a problem: the best thing is to call their office and ask for an appointment. Alternatively, just write to them. Contact details for their local offices are usually listed at the front of the phone directory, although the easiest way to contact all MPs is often at the House of Commons:

Address: House of Commons
             London
             SW1A 0AA
Telephone: 020 7219 3000

Finally, if you happen to be passing while Parliament is sitting, every British citizen has the right to go to the Central Lobby at the House of Commons and ask to see their MP. If the MP is available, he or she is supposed to come and see you.

Do we need a House of Lords?

Some people certainly think we don't – they argue that decisions could be taken by the democratically elected House of Commons on the basis of what the people actually want, and in recent debates about Lords reform this argument has received some support.

Most politicians, however, believe the House of Lords plays a valuable role in the legislative process. They argue that because appointments to the House of Lords are for life, its members are able to take decisions they genuinely believe to be in the country's best interests, free from party political pressure. Also, because no single party has a majority in the Lords, governments have to get a bit of co-operation from the opposition to pass their legislation, thereby making policy making more consensual. Further, the House of Lords contains experts in many areas of policy, and they are able to bring that expertise into the political debate, improving legislation along the way. Finally, although MPs often complain when the Lords block a Bill, they can only block it for a year.

So while we don't strictly need a House of Lords – after all, the Scottish Parliament and the three devolved Assemblies are all unicameral (having just one chamber) – most politicians believe it is useful in improving the quality of the political process.

What is a peer?

'Peer' is another, more general, word for lords and ladies. It includes all the different categories of hereditary aristocracy – dukes, marquesses, earls, viscounts and barons, together with duchesses, marchionesses, countesses, viscountesses and baronesses – as well as people receiving life peerages.

Being made a lord is known as receiving a peerage. However, these days this terminology is all slightly confusing, since recent reforms removed most of the hereditary peers from the House of Lords – it is now possible to be a lord and not sit in the House of Lords. One suggestion to get around this confusion was that members of the House of Lords would be called MLs, rather as members of the Commons are called MPs – but that suggestion wasn't taken up.

How are the Lords appointed?

At the moment, there are two routes: nomination by a political party, or self-nomination via the House of Lords Appointments Commission. Political parties tend to nominate former MPs, senior party figures, or people who have given the party a lot of money. People who get in through the other route have to be very senior in their field, and mustn't be party political – they have to remain independent while in the Lords.

Many people think that the House of Lords is full of, well . . . lords. And in one sense it is – everyone there is either a lord or a lady. However, lords in the traditional sense – those who inherited their title – are rather thin on the ground these days. In fact, after recent reforms just ninety-two of these hereditary peers are still members of the House of Lords. The rest retain their titles, but are no longer members of the United Kingdom Parliament.

One benefit of the current arrangements is that the House of Lords contains people with a great deal of expertise on all sorts of subjects. Most people want to retain this expertise and worry that if the Lords were to be elected, these experts, who are often members of no political party, would never get into the House. This desire to keep some appointed expert members is one reason why elections have not been introduced – there are so many different reform plans that no momentum has built behind any one of them. Those who don't want reform, including many current peers and others who appoint them, such as Tony Blair, have successfully opposed the reform efforts.

Are there different types of Bill?

Once a Bill is passed and becomes an Act, there's no difference between them. However, there are different ways a Bill can be introduced into Parliament.

The majority of Bills introduced are government Bills. Most of these are 'public Bills', affecting public policy.

Private members' Bills are introduced by backbench MPs. They are also public Bills, because they affect public policy. Not all MPs can introduce a private member's Bill – in general they need to come near the top of the annual ballot of MPs to get enough parliamentary time to introduce one. Even then, most don't pass, although there have been notable exceptions, such as the 1967 Abortion Act, introduced by David Steel.

A second way in which MPs can introduce legislation is through a 'ten-minute rule Bill', giving them ten minutes to propose a law. These Bills almost never get further than being introduced, but the mechanism is a good way of raising the profile of an issue.

The final significant type of Bill is a private Bill – totally different from a private member's Bill. These only affect private interests, like a council or a company.

What is secondary legislation?

Secondary legislation actually forms the bulk of our laws. When Parliament passes an Act, it often includes relatively few details about how the Act should be implemented, instead leaving those to the relevant minister. When ministers decide how they wish to implement an Act, they will introduce this secondary legislation, usually in the form of a 'statutory instrument'. Many of these don't get debated in Parliament. Most social security rules are introduced as statutory instruments, for example.

How to pass a law in six (and a half) easy steps

1. A '**Green Paper**' (a consultation paper) is published by the government, with an indication of what it would like to do and asking for people's opinions.
2. A '**White Paper**' is published, saying what the government intends to do. The government sometimes publishes draft Bills so that problems can be ironed out before they're introduced.
3. The Bill is introduced into Parliament. It can start in either the Lords or the Commons, but has to pass all the same stages in both houses before it can become law. The initial stages are the **first reading** (which is just where its name is read out) and the **second reading**, where MPs or Lords get to have a general debate about the main issues in the Bill.
4. Next comes the **committee stage**, where MPs or Lords from all the major parties take several months to consider each clause of the Bill. This is where there is usually the greatest cross-party co-operation and where most amendments are tabled and accepted.
5. At the **report stage**, the committee reports back and the full House of Commons gets to debate the controversial bits. If there are major disagreements

between parties, this is where amendments are brought to important votes. The report stage is followed by the **third reading**, which used to be a general debate on the revised Bill, but nowadays generally means more consideration of specific points, and more amendments.

$5\frac{1}{2}$. **Consideration of amendments**. The Lords and the Commons must pass the same version of a Bill. So if the Lords have passed some changes, this is the stage at which MPs consider the changes and accept or reject them. If they reject them, the Bill goes back to the Lords, where the Lords have the choice of either accepting the MPs' changes or sticking to their guns. If each House keeps rejecting the changes – and this only happens on the most controversial Bills – it's known as 'ping-pong', especially if, as has been known, the Bill bounces backwards and forwards several times in one day.

6. **Royal Assent**. Once they have agreed, the Bill goes to the monarch to be signed, at which point it becomes an Act of Parliament.

Where can people influence what happens to a law?

The depressing truth is there are relatively few opportunities for ordinary people to influence legislation once it is in Parliament, unless they are part of a well-organised lobby demonstrating widespread support for some change.

For ordinary people, their best chance of influencing legislation is normally through their MP. However, even that is no guarantee of success: the life of a backbench MP is often a frustrating one, particularly when governments have large majorities. Governments have a huge amount of power in Parliament and given a reasonable parliamentary majority can normally expect to get pretty much anything they wish passed. Many backbench MPs are regarded by governments as 'lobby fodder' – they'll vote for whatever they're told to vote for. That doesn't mean they are completely without influence, though, and there are a number of ways in which they can affect the process:

- speaking at second reading, or writing to the relevant minister – this is particularly effective if you are in the governing party, because ministers will be more interested in your views;
- getting on the committee considering the Bill and pressing for the change there;
- tabling an amendment;
- influencing a minister on the implementation of a law, when he or she's drafting statutory instruments.

This looks like a pretty short list, but MPs can dramatically increase their influence by working with other MPs and peers with similar views. In this way, they can put pressure on their party leaders to support whatever it is they want to change. Working with people from different parties can help suggest that the point being made is not narrowly party political, and make it easier for the government to concede.

Because of the more independent nature of many members of the House of Lords and the fact that no party has a majority there, it is often easier to get changes made in the second chamber.

Of course, in addition to all this parliamentary activity it's also worthwhile setting up a more widespread lobbying campaign – see Chapter 7 for how to run a lobbying campaign.

Why do MPs sometimes miss votes?

MPs don't spend all their time listening to debates, or voting. Ministers in particular have a huge number of other things to do, but all MPs have other commitments – sitting on committees and meeting constituents, for example – while some even have other jobs. These mean they sometimes have to miss votes, but there are arrangements to allow this to happen.

If an MP needs to miss a vote, they tell their party whips (see the section below for what they do), who then speak to the other parties' whips offices to see if there is another MP who also needs to be away. Pairs are made up of one MP voting for the motion and one voting against it – normally one government and one opposition MP. This system is called 'pairing' and is one of the ways in which the parties work together behind the scenes to make sure business is conducted smoothly.

Why are most MPs still white, middle-aged men?

For one simple reason: at a local level, the political parties nominate comparatively few women or people from ethnic minorities to be their candidates in winnable seats. However, this situation is changing. Since 1997, when Labour introduced all-women shortlists in some safe seats, the number of female Labour MPs has soared – from 33 out of 271 (12 per cent) at the 1992 election to 98 out of 354 (27 per cent) at the 2005 election. Despite its success, this 'positive discrimination' is controversial: both the other parties have tended to object on the basis that any discrimination is wrong, as well as arguing that it is demeaning to women. What's more, it would be hard to use such shortlists to promote every minority. So the other parties are instead looking at other ways of getting local selection panels to choose female and non-white candidates when they put their names forward.

However, despite these moves and the likelihood of further progress, both Houses of Parliament were previously so heavily white and male that they will remain a substantial majority for some time to come.

Some people argue that a substantial increase in the number of women MPs would dramatically alter the conduct of politics by making it more consensual and less antagonistic.

The oath of allegiance

When MPs are elected or re-elected to Parliament, they must take an oath of allegiance. The oath which most MPs take is as follows:

'I .... swear by Almighty God that I will be faithful and bear true allegiance to Her Majesty Queen Elizabeth, her heirs and successors, according to law. So help me God.'

Not all MPs, however, are happy to swear a religious oath, and so in recent years MPs have been able to make a solemn affirmation instead, the wording of which is nevertheless extremely similar:

'I .... do solemnly, sincerely and truly declare and affirm that I will be faithful and bear true allegiance to Her Majesty Queen Elizabeth, her heirs and successors, according to law.'

Obscure as it may seem, the oath of allegiance remains the source of some controversy today, because Sinn Fein MPs refuse either to affirm or to take the oath. This is because Sinn Fein is an Irish republican party, doesn't acknowledge British authority in Northern Ireland and therefore refuses to bear allegiance to the Queen.

Why is Parliament so old fashioned?

Many people, when they hear about how Parliament works, wonder why it remains so old fashioned. In fact, quite a lot of procedures have been modernised in recent years; in particular, those which used to make the place inefficient have been removed. Not everything has been updated, but the odd costumes, forms of address and strange practices at question time have been left alone because they don't slow business down and many MPs from all parties like to keep traditions intact whenever possible.

What does the Speaker do?

The Speaker chairs proceedings in the House of Commons. Although Speakers must be MPs and normally represent a political party, they are elected by all MPs and once they become Speaker they must act independently of any party. They have two responsibilities:

- chairing proceedings in the House of Commons and enforcing its rules;
- defending the independence of the House and representing it in its relations with other bodies.

Most people know about the first of these – the 'Order! Order!' part of the job – but the second is just as important. The Speaker should ensure that backbenchers get a reasonable chance to have their views heard in debates, and that government ministers do not abuse the procedures of the House.

In the House of Lords the Lord Chancellor used to chair debates, but as part of the reforms to the position the Lords will soon be electing a Lord Speaker instead.

What does Black Rod do for the other 364 days of the year?

Once a year the Queen formally opens Parliament; an event known as the State Opening. This is a great ceremonial occasion, with lots of pomp, all the peers in their finery, and the Queen's Speech – written for her by the government and detailing its legislative agenda and political priorities for the coming year.

One of the best-known parts of the ceremony is when a chap called Black Rod (although his full title is Gentleman Usher of the Black Rod) walks through the Palace of Westminster from the House of Lords to the Commons. The doors to the chamber are slammed in his face, and he knocks on them three times to ask MPs to come and hear the Queen's Speech.

The rest of the time, Black Rod is like a parliamentary policeman. He maintains order in the Lords and, together with his opposite number in the Commons (known as the Serjeant at Arms), is responsible for security at the Palace of Westminster. They are also responsible for the other parliamentary buildings, of which there are several – comparatively few MPs have their offices in the Palace of Westminster itself. Most MPs (and peers) have their offices in one of the other buildings nearby.

What is a 'whip' for?

Whips are the political equivalent of school prefects, with the Chief Whip as head girl or boy. Like prefects, they're mainly responsible for maintaining discipline amongst their MPs (or peers), but they also have a valuable role to play in feeding back the views of the troops to their party leadership. The name comes from the whippers-in of foxhounds at a hunt.

Most of a whip's job is pretty uncontroversial – making sure their people get to the vote, and know which way they're voting when they do. Because MPs vote on party lines most of the time, this part of the job isn't normally obvious; it's only on some controversial matters that people rebel against their party leadership.

Most MPs are reluctant to rebel because they were elected as a party representative, but they sometimes will if they very strongly disagree with their party on an issue. That's when the whips earn their money – by cajoling and persuading would-be rebels to vote for their party leadership, or at the very least to stay away from the vote and abstain. The whips' methods vary depending on the MP they're trying to persuade – they'll appeal to the party loyalty of some, offer rewards to others, and some will be threatened with sanctions.

The 'whip' is a weekly bulletin from the Whips' Office which tells MPs when votes are taking place, which way the party is voting on them, and how important it is for them to be there – a three-line whip, the top priority, is literally a vote underlined three times in the bulletin. Withdrawing the whip from an MP or peer is the ultimate sanction, and means suspending them from the party. Whips are not unique to Parliament – most party groups on local councils have them, too.

How do early day motions work?

Early day motions (EDMs) are one of those odd relics which have survived because they serve a useful purpose. MPs sign them to indicate support for a policy or proposal – often calling for government action on some issue. An EDM can't be passed, so the government normally ignores them completely. However, if a single EDM collects several hundred MPs' signatures, it's a good sign that lots of backbench MPs feel strongly about the issue and a sensible government would do well to think about some action on it.

Not all EDMs are serious. MPs use them to congratulate local people in their constituency for some success – football teams winning a tournament, local schools winning a national prize, that sort of thing. MPs love them because they require minimal effort and are a good way of suggesting that they've taken action on something. In fact tabling an EDM is usually just a matter of jotting one down, seeing if some of your colleagues will put their names to it and sending it to the Table Office (where all such things are recorded). Signing one is even easier: most MPs look through the order paper each day to see if there are any good new EDMs listed. If so, they literally sign the page, send it back to the Table Office and, hey presto – a story for their local paper!

How does question time work?

Ministerial question time is another of those occasions which looks very odd to the outside observer – particularly Prime Minister's Question Time every Wednesday, which is the best-known part of the week. Question time allows MPs to hold ministers to account for what their department is up to. They table specific questions a couple of weeks in advance, and are then allowed to ask one 'supplementary' question on the same subject. These supplementary questions are often the questions the MPs really wanted to ask in the first place.

There are a couple of other rules about how it runs:

1. Questions alternate between government backbenchers and opposition MPs. The Speaker tries to keep a reasonable balance between MPs from all parties.

2. The shadow minister and Liberal Democrat spokesman don't have to table questions – they are always allotted a couple of questions.

3. You often see MPs bobbing up and down. They're trying to catch the Speaker's eye to indicate that they want to ask an extra question on the current subject. They haven't tabled questions themselves but still want to be called.

Parliamentary language

People get very confused about the language used in Parliament. However, there are a few simple rules about what they're allowed to say – and not to say:

1. MPs mustn't address one another directly, but rather via the Speaker. For example, 'Mr Speaker, would the Prime Minister tell the House . . .'

2. They mustn't use any abusive language, and on no account must they ever accuse another MP of lying.

3. MPs have something called 'parliamentary privilege', which allows them to say things in Parliament that would be libellous if said outside. This freedom of speech dates from the 1689 Bill of Rights, and although it is rarely used, MPs do occasionally do so, normally to raise serious issues.

What did they say?

Honourable	Every MP is known as 'an Honourable Member'
Right Honourable	Members of the Privy Council (see Chapter 2) are referred to as 'Right Honourable'
. . . and Learned	MPs who were previously or still are barristers
. . . and Gallant	Used very rarely these days, but an MP who is either a serving

	military officer or a senior retired officer
Honourable Friend	When speaking to or of an MP of the same party
Another place	The House of Lords – MPs aren't allowed to refer to it by name!

What do committees do?

There are three main types of committee in Parliament:

- select committees – permanent committees which keep track of government policy and how departments are run
- standing committees – temporary committees which examine Bills in detail when they're being considered by Parliament
- backbench committees – permanent committees which allow MPs from a particular party to meet and discuss party policy on an issue.

Of these, select committees are probably the most important. They are normally chaired by a member of the government, but contain members from all the major parties. They keep an eye both on a given area of policy and on how well a particular government department is run. For example, the Transport Committee will have hearings at which it examines government policy, how well money is being spent and how well the various transport agencies are being run. Select committee reports are normally unanimous, which gives them added weight: ministers find it hard to dismiss critical reports because they have the backing of MPs from all parties. In recent years there have been efforts to increase the power of select committees as a balance against the increasing power of the government.

Most select committees are departmental – covering a particular department – but others have a broader remit. Of these, the Public Accounts Committee, which reports on how well public money is being spent, is the most important. Its reports are usually based on findings from the National Audit Office (NAO), which scrutinises the accounts of all government departments, agencies and other public bodies. Because their work is so thorough, NAO reports have a big impact.

One final type of committee is the all-party group. These less formal groups allow MPs and peers from all parties to meet and discuss, and sometimes lobby for changes on, issues of common interest. There are more than 250 such groups – covering everything from abuse investigations to youth hostelling. In addition to these, there are more than 100 all-party country groups, which MPs and peers tend to join to express friendship for a particular country.

Two committees don't fit into any category:

- The Intelligence and Security Committee (ISC), which oversees the 'secret state'. Although its members are MPs and peers, they are all appointed by the Prime Minister – making it very different to a normal select committee.
- The Committee on Standards in Public Life, which provides recommendations about ethical standards in public life. Like the ISC, its members are appointed by the Prime Minister.

How much money do MPs make?

Not as much as you'd think. Their actual salary is about £59,000 a year (although ministers are paid a ministerial salary on top of that – see Chapter 2). As well as their salary, they can claim their travel expenses on parliamentary business, their office costs are also paid for, and if their constituency is outside London they get an extra £21,000 to pay the costs of staying in the city.

On top of that, many MPs earn extra money outside Parliament. More often than not, it's a couple of hundred quid a year for some TV appearances, which they often give to charity. But some earn a lot extra. For example, in 2005 William Hague earned more than £685,000 from giving speeches, writing a column for the *News of the World*, writing a biography of William Pitt the Younger, being a company director and advising some other companies.

Many people believe that MPs are paid a decent whack to be an MP, and they should concentrate on that. Others reply that Parliament benefits from MPs with experience of the world outside politics.

The other concern is whether this money influences the decisions they take. This is the main reason the Register of Members' Interests was set up. MPs must declare interests worth more than 1 per cent of their salary – £590. If they want to speak in the House of Commons on a subject in which they have a financial interest, they must declare that interest before they speak.

How can politicians be held to account?

The British parliamentary system offers quite a number of ways in which politicians can be held accountable between elections – certainly more than in other systems. Ministers, for example, have to face:

- regular question time sessions in the House of Commons;
- appearances before select committees;
- grillings in media interviews.

They also have to abide by the rules laid out in the Ministerial Code. The code has two sections – one regulating ministers' ethical conduct, the other procedures in government. Several recent ministerial resignations – including Beverley Hughes in 2004 and David Blunkett in 2005 – were the result of transgressing various parts of the code. An important part of this document is the seven principles of public life, developed by the Committee on Standards in Public Life (see the section on different committees above). The seven principles are:

- selflessness
- integrity
- objectivity
- accountability
- openness
- honesty
- leadership.

If ministers are found to have made really serious mistakes, either breaching the code or cocking up a policy, their fate rests in the hands of the Prime Minister. There will probably be a great hue and cry calling for their resignation, but in reality ministers rarely resign unless the mistake is extremely serious or their continued presence is badly damaging the rest of the government. In those circumstances the 'resignation' may not be entirely voluntary.

For other politicians, and for many ministers, the real reckoning comes at election time: elections are the ultimate accountability mechanism. They give voters the opportunity to mull over the record of both their MP and his or her party. It's at this point that the party manifesto – a document containing all that party's promises – is particularly useful. Many voters take the opportunity at election time to look back on the promises made in the last manifesto to see if they were kept.

What happens to MPs when they leave Parliament?

Being an MP or a minister is pretty insecure. Every time there's an election, they risk losing their job and career. What's more, unlike many other careers, when people tend to get sacked because they're doing a bad job, MPs and ministers can often be thrown out regardless of their individual performance.

To reflect this insecurity, there is a package of assistance available. For a start, MPs get some money to help them wind down their parliamentary offices gradually, while ministers get a large lump sum when they leave office. The parliamentary pension is also generous, so they won't be hard up when they retire.

However, they are still faced with making ends meet. Many of them decide to make use of their knowledge of politics and get jobs as lobbyists, consultants or advisers. Ministers are banned from taking jobs with companies in areas for which they were recently responsible, but generally the bans only last for a year or so. That means energy ministers often end up working in the energy sector, and so on. Some senior MPs get peerages and continue their political careers in the House of Lords. A smaller number return to the careers they had before going into politics, and others retire.

5

Political parties

Most parliamentary activity takes place within the context of political parties. These slightly odd bodies bring together people with sometimes quite different political views to co-operate for their mutual benefit. The discipline they impose on their members both provides opportunities and imposes limitations on their freedom of manoeuvre. It makes parties some of the most powerful institutions in British politics.

Do we need political parties?

We do, really. Although some political systems operate without them – the legislature in the US state of Nebraska, for example – political parties play an important part in most democratic systems.

They are vital in bringing together (mostly) like-minded groups of people to seek power and achieve their common political aims. Those different groups co-operate to develop a common agenda, which they can then implement once in power. Without the organisation and discipline which parties provide, the political system would be chaotic – constantly having to find compromises from amongst literally hundreds of representatives on every issue. Voters would also have a difficult time choosing between their many different options.

Modern parties emerged in the mid–nineteenth century, when the number of people eligible to vote increased dramatically, and over the last hundred years they have gradually grown more organised and disciplined. That discipline is sometimes a burden – in recent years more independent-minded members of all political parties have sometimes found it grating – but some degree of discipline is necessary to ensure the common agenda is implemented.

Most major parties have three tiers of involvement:

- leadership – usually MPs and peers, but also senior people in the party structure;
- activists – often regarded as holding the strongest views in the party, they feel strongly enough about matters to give up their free time for the cause;
- members – not quite passionate enough to be active in the party, but they support it enough to join and help fund its activities.

Because parties contain so many people who feel passionately about political issues, they often have pretty vigorous internal debates about what the party policy should be on any given subject. This is particularly so within the leadership, where there are often strong disagreements between different factions – over both policies and personalities. It is sometimes said that in any political party your opponents are in front of you (i.e. the opposition parties) while your enemies are behind you. In most parties, there is also a good deal of tension between the leadership and the activists – the latter often complaining if the leadership makes ideological compromises in order to try and attract the support of more moderate voters. These often come out at party conferences, which normally take place twice a year – smaller affairs in the spring and large, televised, week-long political conventions in Britain's seaside resorts in the autumn.

Where did the parties come from?

Conservatives: The Conservatives (or 'Tories', as they were once and are still sometimes known) have been one of two major parties since the early nineteenth century. Throughout the period they have been on the centre-right of the British political spectrum, and are by far the most successful of the three major parties. In fact their domination of the twentieth century was such that it was christened by some the 'Conservative Century'. From the late nineteenth century until the early 1970s the prevailing political ideology was 'one-nation Conservatism', which was generally taken to mean policies which united the nation. In 1975, Margaret Thatcher's election as party leader signalled the start of a far harder-nosed set of policies – one designed to rid the country of its economic ills. The earlier ideology fell by the wayside and Conservatives today continue to wrestle with the intellectual and political heritage of both traditions.

Labour: The Labour Party was formed, in stages, around the turn of the twentieth century, by trade unions and existing socialist parties. It initially supported the Liberal Party, and the first two Labour governments didn't have proper House of Commons majorities and failed to achieve much. In 1945, the first full Labour government was elected and carried out a radical programme of nationalisation and construction of the welfare state. From the mid-1960s, the party moved steadily to the left, and its 1983 general election manifesto was so left wing it was described by one of its own MPs as 'the longest suicide note in history'. Reforming leaders moved Labour steadily back towards the centre-left of British politics and in 1997 it won its first general election for twenty-three years.

Liberal Democrats: The modern heirs to a long political

tradition. In the nineteenth and early twentieth century, the Liberal Party emerged from the 'Whigs' to be the main centre-left party in British politics. Between 1906 and 1922 the party enacted some major social reforms but then split, and was largely replaced by the Labour Party. The Liberals nearly disappeared altogether in the 1950s, but a decade later began rebuilding. In the 1980s a fourth party, the Social Democratic Party (SDP), was formed by defectors from Labour, and in 1988 the two parties merged to form the Liberal Democrats. They are on the centre-left of British politics, but with a more libertarian streak than Labour.

Scottish National Party (SNP): The SNP was formed in the early twentieth century and campaigns for an independent Scotland. Its electoral highpoint was the 1970s, but it has been revived by devolution and is now the main opposition party in the Scottish Parliament.

Plaid Cymru: Plaid Cymru is the Welsh nationalist party, wanting Wales to be independent. Plaid has received electoral support mainly from the Welsh-speaking north of Wales, and support for the Welsh language has always been a major goal. Following devolution, Plaid has been the main opposition party in the Welsh Assembly.

What's the difference between Old and New Labour?

In a sentence, 'Old Labour' is left wing and pro-union; 'New Labour' is centre-left and pro-market.

'New Labour' was a name given to the Labour Party by Tony Blair when he took over in 1994. He wanted to make clear that under his leadership the party was different from the one that had suffered four consecutive election defeats.

Modelled on the 'New Democrats' in the United States, the name change was intended to symbolise a more centrist party willing to ditch some of Labour's old attachments. This shift was symbolised in the battle to reform Clause 4 of the party's constitution. Where the old one, written in 1918, had called for extensive nationalisation, the new one said that Labour

> believes that by the strength of our common endeavour we achieve more than we achieve alone, so as to create for each of us the means to realise our true potential and for all of us a community in which power, wealth and opportunity are in the hands of the many, not the few.

Such language came to symbolise 'New Labour'. And although the characterisations are sometimes crude, the old/new divide remains the key ideological fault line in the Labour Party today.

Where do political parties get their money from?

This depends on the political party, and it's important to distinguish between the national parties (which tend to depend more on large donations) and local parties (which often get most money from their members – in quite small sums). It's also difficult to put a firm figure on the proportion coming from each source, because it changes each year, and all donations tend to peak around an election. But in general:

- The Conservatives get most of their money from quite a small number of very wealthy donors. They used to get a lot from businesses, but business donations fell away when

69

the rules on political donations were changed. A relatively small share of their income comes from normal party members. Quite a lot comes from the 'Short money' made available to opposition parties (see box on stage funding below).

- Labour gets a great deal from the trade unions, although this amount has gone down a lot with the party's move towards the centre. Nowadays much of its income comes in the form of large donations from a few wealthy donors and, like the Conservatives, a relatively small share comes from normal party members.
- The Liberal Democrats are the most reliant on small donations from their members. However, at the 2005 general election they received their largest ever donation – £2.4 million from a single wealthy individual. Between elections they rely heavily on Short money.

Labour and the Conservatives usually raise and spend roughly equivalent amounts of money, with the Liberal Democrats getting far less and the other parties negligible amounts by comparison. Although there is now a limit to how much can be spent in election campaigns, it is so high that it does not constrain the larger parties' spending – some people argue that this gives those parties an unfair advantage.

In recent years, the rules about donating to political parties have tightened. All significant donations now have to be declared publicly; only British people and British companies can make donations in Britain; and it's harder for businesses to give money. These rules are all intended to open the process up and allay concerns about corruption.

Do financial backers call the tune – how important are they to parties?

Very important – during the 2005 general election, the three major parties received a large proportion of their income from just a handful of big donors. Without that money they could not have afforded to run such extensive campaigns.

Donors do benefit from giving money, but it's not clear exactly to what extent. They generally get invited to social functions with senior party figures, and their access is generally better than for normal party members. There are occasional scandals about donations in exchange for specific policies apparently being amended – as in 1997 when Bernie Ecclestone, the boss of Formula 1 motor racing, donated £1 million to Labour and the party's policy on tobacco advertising in F1 was changed shortly afterwards. Labour furiously denied there had been any connection and returned the £1 million, but the suspicion remained.

Almost as controversial is the question of honours. Some observers worry how many peerages big donors get, in many cases without other obvious factors in their favour. It certainly hasn't got as bad as it was in the early 1920s, when the 'honours scandal' revealed that David Lloyd George had been openly selling honours. Nevertheless, honours are supposed to reward merit, not wealth, and there are concerns about the corruption of the system. No surprise, perhaps, that some people want to remove any taint of corruption by funding parties from taxation instead (see box below).

Should there be state funding of political parties?

There already is some state funding. In recognition of the important constitutional role they play in challenging and scrutinising the government, opposition parties in the

House of Commons are eligible for something called 'Short money'. This varies depending on how many MPs a party has; the total amount available has risen quite substantially in recent years and is now worth £5.5m.

There are two reasons for state funding – to equalise how much the parties receive and to remove any suspicion that money is a corrupting influence in politics. Nevertheless there is limited political support for full-scale state funding for political parties. Opponents argue that contributing to a political party should remain voluntary – if people agree with a party they can support it but if they don't their taxes shouldn't go towards it. They also argue that the money could be better spent.

How do the parties talk to each other?

Politics is sometimes presented as being so antagonistic that it comes close to being a contact sport. Some people argue that the design of the House of Commons, with two sides facing each other, heightens tensions and makes it look to the public like they're enemies. The parties do challenge one another vigorously, but MPs and peers from all parties just as often have to work together to get things done.

First of all, many MPs from different parties will have known one another before entering Parliament, or had friends in common, and many friendships are formed through working together on various matters – sitting on committees, for example.

Second, many of the committees force inter-party co-operation. This is particularly true of select committees, whose reports are normally unanimous. MPs and peers also work closely together on all-party groups, which are explicitly non-partisan (hence the name).

Third, the parties need to speak together to organise business. This is especially important for the smaller parties, so that their interests aren't ignored in Parliament, and is done through a system called the 'usual channels' – which really just means the parties' whips' offices.

Finally, the government sometimes needs to brief the opposition parties on important matters. This happens on issues such as Northern Ireland and terrorism, where there is greater cross-party co-operation anyway. These briefings are normally on 'Privy Council terms' (see Chapter 2). In a similar way, opposition parties are able to receive extensive briefings from senior civil servants in the run-up to a general election. This arrangement is designed to ensure that if they win, they have some idea what to expect when they take office.

6

For God and King

What does the Queen actually do?

The Queen is the monarch and the head of state, a position which might best be described as the chief public representative of Britain.

It's a slightly odd job. Monarchs once had extremely wide-ranging powers, and in theory government is still carried out in the Queen's name. However, Britain today is a constitutional monarchy, and the monarch's powers are limited. Her political role is tightly circumscribed: she must be completely impartial politically and isn't even allowed to express political views in public.

The ceremonial role as head of state is still important, though. Most visibly this includes 'embodying the nation' in times of difficulty or of celebration. More often it means an endless series of engagements around the country, meeting the people and celebrating local and national achievements. The Queen's patronage of numerous charities is a part of this role, which she shares with other members of the royal family.

The Queen has four further roles, but all are more ceremonial than substantial:

- head of the armed forces, although she can't declare war;
- Supreme Governor of the Church of England, but she has no role in doctrinal matters and her role in appointments is a formal one alone; she is also 'Defender of the Faith' but,

confusingly, this is formally unrelated to the Church of England;

- head of the Commonwealth, although her political role here is circumscribed and it has its own secretariat;
- head of state of some Commonwealth countries, including Australia, Canada and New Zealand.

Does the Queen have any political role?

She does, but it is extremely limited – convention even dictates that she doesn't vote in elections. Mostly, her powers are 'formal' rather than 'operational'. There is still debate about just two of her formal powers: appointing the Prime Minister and calling an election. The question is whether she could influence who would be appointed Prime Minister, and whether she could refuse a PM's request to call an election.

Certainly, neither power would be used in normal circumstances. However, some constitutional scholars argue that there are situations in which the Queen might have a role in choosing a Prime Minister, although there are very few situations in which she would refuse to call an election. This argument is based on three constitutional understandings:

- the Queen's government must be carried on;
- the Prime Minister must be able to command a majority in the House of Commons;
- the Prime Minister must be able to lead or get the support of the majority party in the House of Commons.

Situations where the Queen might be involved include a hung parliament, where no party has a majority, or where a Prime Minister dies in office and there is no obvious successor. Yet the other side of the Queen's political impartiality is that politicians aren't supposed to embarrass her, or force her to take a political view. So even in one of these situations, party leaders understand that they must resolve any problems amongst themselves.

Because this whole area of the British constitution is shrouded in secrecy and such situations will be unique, no one really knows what would happen.

Formal powers which aren't really powers
- Signing Bills from Parliament
- Royal prerogative powers (see Chapter 2 for these)
- Giving the Queen's Speech at the opening of a new Parliament (see Chapter 4)
- Awards and peerages (although there is personal discretion over some)

The Queen is required to take the government's advice on all other political matters. For example, the Queen's Speech is written by ministers (or their advisers), she can't reject recommendations for the vast majority of honours (a very few are personal to her) and she has to invite heads of state for formal visits when the government asks her to. In 1978, she was reportedly very unhappy about being 'asked' to invite the Romanian dictator Nicolae Ceauşescu.

So what political powers remain? Really just the three rights described by the constitutional expert Walter Bagehot back in the nineteenth century: 'the right to be consulted, the right to encourage, the right to warn'. The Queen remains in close touch with politics, reading many government papers and holding a weekly 'audience' with the Prime Minister. Although this is one of the most secret areas of the constitution, she does occasionally make use of her rights to encourage or to warn. Because of her long experience and famous discretion, many Prime Ministers have found their weekly audiences useful for discussing thorny matters.

What about other members of the royal family?

In political and constitutional terms, they matter only if they might one day become monarch. So the distant cousins' only other roles are the vital ones of charity work and appearing in the society pages of *Tatler* magazine!

When the Queen dies, it is assumed that Prince Charles will become King and will take on all the responsibilities which go with the title. Only the role as head of the Commonwealth, which has only come into existence in its present form under Elizabeth II, is in any doubt. And although Charles would probably be considered for the job, he may well not get it. Charles has also indicated that he would prefer to be a 'defender of faiths', rather than Defender of *the* Faith (my italics), which would be more a semantic than a constitutional change.

How much does all this cost?

Under a deal struck between King George III and the government, revenue from the Crown Lands goes to the government and in return the monarch receives a set amount of money from the public purse – this is known as the 'civil list' and currently stands at just over £10m a year. It pays for the costs of staff and running the royal household. Nowadays this money pays both for the Queen and for a number of other members of the royal family.

The Queen also receives money from the Department for Culture, Media and Sport to help pay for the upkeep of the royal palaces, and from the Department for Transport (DfT) for her travel needs. In recent years various economies have dramatically reduced the amount required from the DfT, but together the three budgets add up to £37m a year (in 2004/05).

If we didn't have a monarch, is the only alternative really a US-style president?

Because virtually all government business is currently conducted in the name of the Queen, any move away from our present constitutional monarchy to a republic would be a major step, requiring substantial alterations to the constitutional architecture.

But moving to a US-style presidency would require such extensive alterations that it would be more akin to rebuilding the whole constitution. This is because the Americans have an executive presidency, which wraps together the roles of head of state (our monarch) and head of government (our Prime Minister). There seems to be very little appetite for such a move in this country.

Still, many people would like to see an elected head of state because they object to the lack of democracy in our current arrangements. A more popular model for many of these republicans is a non-political presidency, where the main role is ceremonial – embodying the nation and so on. The only residual political commitments would be appointing the government. Many countries already have such a head of state, amongst them Ireland, Germany and Israel.

What does the Church of England do?

The Church of England is the 'established' church in England, just as the Church of Scotland is the 'established' church in Scotland (although the Queen is not Supreme Governor of the Church of Scotland). Wales and Northern Ireland don't have established churches.

Being 'established' means that it is the nation's official

church. Today it means little for most people, but for hundreds of years it meant discrimination, and sometimes outright persecution, for people who were not Anglicans. Some of that discrimination remains – for example, a Catholic still cannot become monarch.

There are few remaining connections between Church and state. The most important are that bishops are appointed by the Queen (although the Prime Minister 'advises' her on who to appoint) and that senior bishops receive seats in the House of Lords.

The Church has its own parliament, called the General Synod. It shares responsibility with the Westminster Parliament for organisational measures affecting the Church, but doctrinal matters are normally dealt with by the synod alone. The synod's three houses – the House of Bishops, the House of Clergy and the House of Laity – represent the church's hierarchy.

And what about the Archbishop of Canterbury?

The Archbishop of Canterbury is the religious head of the Church of England ('Primate of All England') and head of the Anglican Communion – the wider collection of Anglican churches, with about seventy million members around the world.

He is entitled to sit in the House of Lords, and still comes above everyone except the Royal Family in the constitutional order of precedence, including even the Prime Minister. This order of precedence is only of ceremonial importance and doesn't signify real power.

Could the Church of England be disestablished?

It could. And unlike abolishing the monarchy, this would only mean tinkering with lots of pieces of law, because the Church is mentioned in many of them, rather than wholesale renovation of the constitution. But there is little demand for such a change, perhaps, paradoxically, because the Church of England has ceased to play a central role in the nation's affairs.

But the movement to disestablish the church has produced one semi-notable fact. The word meaning 'opposition to disestablishment' – 'antidisestablishmentarianism' – is amongst the longest words in the English language.

So where do other churches, and religions, fit in?

Nowhere, formally: neither other Christian denominations nor other religions have any formal position. And although the leaders of different faiths have recently been given peerages, and can therefore sit in the House of Lords, they are not entitled to them by virtue of their position. What's more, they are still totally outnumbered by the twenty-six Church of England bishops.

7
Public opinion, the media and lobbying

Much has changed in British politics over the last fifty years. Many of the changes are described elsewhere in this book – the increasing power of the Prime Minister, the decline of Parliament, greater openness in government and devolution, to name just a few. But the growing power and broadening role of the media – particularly television – has in turn affected all of these other changes. In truth it is hard to exaggerate how far the media influence politics – everything from leading public opinion to influencing the decision-making processes of government.

This chapter also looks at polling – the main way politicians now hear public views – and lobbying, the way in which special interests get their voices heard in the corridors of power. It asks whether, with falling membership of political parties, charities and pressure groups are the new vehicles for mass participation in politics.

How important are the media in politics?

Since the messenger can affect the message, extremely important. After all, 'media' is simply the plural of 'medium', the means by which something is transmitted – in this case information about politics. No media equals very little information about politics. This puts the media at the very centre of the political world, with a vital role to play in Britain's democratic life. Without free media, the public would not be able to get the accurate information about political life they need. As a result, political parties are very keen to make sure the political news and information carried in the media are favourable to them. Some observers worry that this trend has gone so far that the media implications are now considered at a very early stage of a policy's development – and that press spokesmen and spin doctors have too much influence on policy, particularly in government.

There are, though, competing theories about how far the media actually affect public opinion – this field offers rich pickings for media studies departments. Most of the theories, though, accept that the media influence politics in some ways, mainly through:

- the agenda – influencing what people think *about* (and what they don't);
- framing – influencing *how* they think about political issues;
- direct effects – newspapers influencing the way their readers vote, for example. In 1992 the *Sun* claimed that it won the election for John Major's Conservatives through just this route, but there is little evidence for the claim.

Some theorists disagree with all this. They argue that the media merely reinforce opinions which people already have – meaning Conservative voters are more likely to buy the *Daily Mail*, for example, or Labour voters the *Guardian*. As with many social science theories, there is probably some truth in all of them.

How do politicians influence the media?

Politicians want the media to do three things – carry stories favourable to them, pass over stories unfavourable to them, and carry their view of the stories which are already running. This is not an inherently bad thing – in fact in a democracy it's a perfectly reasonable goal. Indeed with a vast amount of media space now available to be filled, it's no surprise that politicians want it filled with their message, and not the message from the other side.

They use all sorts of techniques to do so, from daily press initiatives to complicated marketing and communication strategies. So important has publicity become that the media implications are now considered from the very beginning of policy development. One tried and trusted way of doing this is to float an idea in a speech or interview to gauge public reaction: only if that reaction is positive will the policy be developed further. And once the policy has been agreed, the media relations effort is meticulously planned, too. Since 1997, the Labour government has operated something called 'the grid', which co-ordinates the press initiatives from every part of government to ensure that its members don't speak at cross-purposes.

Media relations have become a constant battle for public attention and public opinion. That battle has been complicated by the birth of rolling news channels such as Sky News, BBC News 24 and CNN, creating a 24-hour news cycle. Because journalists always want to be reporting on a new story, not covering the same one for several days (it's called 'news' for a reason, after all), there's constant pressure to 'move the story on'. So the news cycle has become increasingly short and politicians, if they want their message to fill that media space, need to move with the story.

There is one area, however, where politicians are reluctant to go in their search for media coverage. Compared to other countries, British politicians don't spend a lot of money on advertising. This is for two reasons:

- Advertisements in newspapers and magazines are very expensive, and since political parties in Britain don't have huge resources they generally can't afford to advertise except at election time.
- Parties are banned from advertising on television. Instead they get a certain number of free 'party political broadcasts' (and at election time 'party election broadcasts') on each of the main television channels. The number they are entitled to depends on past election performance, how many candidates they are putting forward, and current opinion polling; this is designed to stop people (like publicity seekers) from abusing the system in order to get what amounts to free advertising space, although some of the small parties complain that it's also unfair to them.

So what's 'spin'?

'Spin' is the increasingly pejorative term for media manipulation. Putting your own spin on a story originally meant reinterpreting the agreed facts, or offering different facts to present a more favourable case. But more recently it has come to be associated with twisting the facts and in extreme cases presenting a picture which is actually false.

Some of the criticism levelled at 'spin doctors' is unfair – as noted above, it is perfectly legitimate for politicians or parties to present their view of the facts – but there is a clear line between that and lying.

In a spin – Jo Moore has a bad day

On the afternoon of 11 September 2001, people around the world were watching with horror as terrorists attacked New York and Washington. But looking at the same pictures in the Department of Transport, Jo Moore, a Labour Party special adviser and spin doctor, instead saw an opportunity. Since the following day's papers would be full of stories about the terrorist attacks, she reasoned, wouldn't it be a good time to release some information the government knew would be badly received? She wrote an e-mail suggesting that it would be 'a very good day to get out anything we want to bury'.

For many people, this story epitomised the cynicism of spin: politicians profiting from tragedy, the government trying to conceal information the public had a right to know, unelected spin doctors run amok. Jo Moore apologised and kept her job, although she was to resign just months later. But the damage to public trust in politicians had been done.

Do the media trivialise politics?

Politicians are certainly fond of complaining about it, and at times it's probably true. Certainly the number of times you hear or see 'boring' attached to a discussion isn't healthy for politics. And part of the effort to reconnect with readers, listeners and viewers has seen politics becoming ever more personalised, as though it were another strand of celebrity, with party leaders looming ever larger and discussion about whether a politician likes briefs or boxers, or what type of shoes they wear, sometimes generating as much coverage as their views on the economy or pension reform.

But that isn't quite the whole story. Politicians must share some of the blame for these developments. Clumsy news management, a refusal to open the political process and the ethical shortcomings of some have all contributed to perception problems amongst the public. And while the media's efforts to cover politics in new ways haven't always worked, sometimes they have; meanwhile politicians as a class have often proved a formidable barrier to the way politics is seen. Furthermore, the parties are complicit in the personalisation – consciously promoting party leaders at the expense of other senior figures and encouraging coverage of them as 'people', not just politicians. So, as with so many of the questions in this book, the answer is closest to six of one and half a dozen of the other.

Is there anything the media don't report?

Yes – and it revolves around something called 'the lobby'. All the top political reporters are members of the lobby. They are allowed privileged access into the Members' Lobby of the House of Commons – hence 'lobby' – and receive off-the-record briefings, particularly from the government. The key lobby rule is that briefings are non-attributable – you don't name your source.

Until fairly recently the lobby's daily briefings from the government were highly secretive, and the system was some-times criticised for producing a too-close relationship between the media and government. Since 1986, though, when the newly founded *Independent* refused to take part (it later relented), this part of the lobby system has broken down, and in 2002 the daily briefings were placed on the record. However, 'lobby rules' still apply in dealings with MPs, and many other government briefings still take place 'off the record'. This sometimes leads to the ridiculous situation of a politician denying on the record what he or she is perfectly prepared to admit off the record.

If journalists have a story not covered by lobby rules, in general they only hold it back if it might lead to some legal action or if the story will breach one of the various codes which they have to abide by. For example, both the Press Complaints Commission (for newspapers and magazines) and Ofcom (for broadcasters) strictly limit the stories which journalists can run about the children of public figures. Legal action is sometimes taken by public figures trying to prevent a story from being covered, but the government also takes legal action to prevent the publication of secret information. This is usually done through a court injunction.

However, journalists must also bear in mind the risk of being sued, and that can stop stories being run. The risk of self-censorship is worsened by the way the libel laws in Britain work. In some other countries, if a journalist is sued for libel, it is the responsibility of the claimant to demonstrate it; in Britain the burden lies entirely with the journalist to prove their truthfulness.

In the past, journalists were a lot more reluctant to run stories on politicians' private lives. There was a widespread feeling that what politicians did in private didn't affect the way they did their jobs in public, and therefore it wasn't relevant. All sorts of stories were held back which today would be too juicy for newspaper editors to avoid.

The *Daily Express* changes sides

In 2001, the *Daily Express* backed the Labour Party to win that year's general election. It was an extraordinary development – the *Express* had historically been on the right of British politics, and had backed the Conservatives at every general election in living memory.

The switch was due to changes in ownership. It had begun in 1998, when Lord Hollick had become proprietor of the Express Group, appointed a new, liberal editorial team and consciously pushed the paper in a centrist direction.

There was little demand for a reversal when the *Express* was sold again, in 2000, to the magazine proprietor Richard Desmond. Desmond was personally sympathetic to Labour (he donated £100,000 to the party in 2001) and wanted to back the winning party in the election. He did, but the new orientation was to prove short lived.

By 2004 the paper switched back, angered by the government's decision to hold a referendum on the EU constitution after the election rather than before. In truth, though, the paper had always been uncomfortable sitting in the political centre, and had been following a more right-wing agenda for some time; the reverse switch was hardly a surprise. The new editor, Peter Hill, claimed that the decision was entirely his, but most industry-watchers thought Desmond had had a substantial say in the decision.

How does a newspaper choose its allegiance?

British newspapers are unusual in being so overtly political. For many of them, this editorial line is strongly reflected in their news coverage – even if the two are nominally separate. The tabloids are particularly prone to this, with front page editorials, campaigning journalism and politically led news.

How a newspaper chooses its allegiance depends on the paper, but is usually influenced by one or more of three factors:

- Who owns it – if they have a strong political view personally, this will often dictate a newspaper's editorial line. Rupert Murdoch is particularly renowned for the tight grip he keeps on his papers' political affiliations (see also box above).

- Who edits it – the editor, and sometimes the political editor, can be very influential.
- Who reads it – however strongly the owner and editor feel about something, newspapers are businesses, and if the readers object to a particular editorial line and the paper loses sales, there's a good chance the line will be changed.

Who did the papers support in 2005?

	Party supported in 2005
Tabloids	
Daily Express	Conservative
Daily Mail	Conservative
Daily Mirror	Labour
Sun	Labour
Broadsheets	
Daily Telegraph	Conservative
Financial Times	Labour
Guardian	Labour
Independent	anti-Conservative
Times	Labour

Why does so much get leaked to the press?

Things generally get leaked because somebody with access to private information wants to damage either someone (normally a colleague, rival or boss) or something (often a policy, another department or government).

While leaks appear all the time, only occasionally are they really significant, like the leaking, just before the 2005 general election, of the Attorney General's legal advice on the Iraq war.

For major leaks like this, governments often set up an inquiry, but the source is rarely found. Yet for the majority of leaks – more often than not just tittle-tattle about who said what to whom – a bit of basic detective work will give a good idea of who was responsible. Asking what was leaked, to whom, who had access to it, and who benefited from the leak will usually get pretty close to the mark.

Politicians complain that leaks inhibit free discussion – if they're always worried that something will appear on the front page of the papers, they can't be so frank in expressing their real views, including their doubts. It is a concern, and the same argument is used against publishing memoirs and diaries. Yet in reality leaking is now so pervasive that many politicians just assume someone else will do it if they don't, so they'd better get in first. In the 1960s leaking became so bad that Prime Minister Harold Wilson had to ask his ministers to stop it. What rather undermined this high-minded request was that he'd leaked the news to a friendly journalist before he had spoken to them!

Do opinion polls actually work?

They do, which means everyone in politics – politicians them-selves, pressure groups, lobbyists and the media – find them very interesting.

The theory behind polls is called 'sampling theory' and fortunately you don't need a degree in maths to understand how it works.

Imagine you have 1,000 ping-pong balls in a bag – 500 black and 500 white. If you choose 100 at random, sampling theory says you are likely to get about fifty of each. What's more, if you keep choosing sets of 100 balls, you're likely to get roughly the same result. Why?

Think of each set of 100 choices. The chance of getting any set of choices (e.g. white, black, black, black, white etc.) in exactly that order is 1 in 600,000,000,000,000,000,000,000,000,000,000 – very bad odds. Those are also exactly the odds on getting 100 white balls, because only one set of choices will get all white balls.

But the odds of getting ninety-nine white balls and one black are much better. There are 100 different 'sets' of 99 white and 1 black, because it doesn't matter when the black ball is chosen – it could come first, second, third, fourth (and so on). The closer to 50-50 the end result, the more sets of choices which could produce that result.

There are literally millions of different ways of getting fifty balls of each colour, and so the odds reduce very dramatically – so dramatically, in fact, that they are just 1 in 1.25.

So looking at a relatively small sample should produce an accurate picture of the whole. It's vital, though, that the sample is large enough for the operation to work properly, but once it is the polls should be broadly accurate, and the same principles will apply whether you're polling voting intentions or preferences for pop stars.

People who are interviewed for polls are normally chosen at random, while the polls themselves can be conducted in a number of different ways, mostly face to face or over the telephone (although one company now does polling over the internet). The most widely used system is telephone polling, where numbers can be dialled at random.

Once they have the collected the data, most polling companies weight the samples. They do this in different ways, but they all do it to compensate for unbalanced samples. For example, if an unweighted sample included far more Liverpudlians than exist in the general population, the poll might show Steven Gerrard is the best midfielder in the world; if the bias was towards west Londoners, the conclusion might be that Frank Lampard is best. Pollsters try to balance out these differences by attaching more value to the opinions of under-represented groups in a poll.

Some good 'poll etiquette'

Some polls are better than others. Here are five easy ways to make sure you understand what they're saying:

1. Compare like with like. Because polling companies have different methodologies the results aren't really comparable.
2. Look at when the sampling was done. The media sometimes breathlessly report that a poll shows public support has held up after a scandal the previous day, when the polling was done three days ago.
3. Look at the sample size. Most political polls in Britain use samples of more than 1,000, a decent number.
4. Check the margin of error. If a poll suggesting 40 per cent of people like apples has a 5 per cent margin of error, anywhere between 35 per cent and 45 per cent of people could actually like apples. Generally, a bigger sample size means a smaller margin of error.
5. Make sure you know what you're looking at – some polls on voting indication only include 'likely' voters, not all voters.

Should we worry about lobbying?

Not necessarily. As with many parts of political life described in this book, there's nothing inherently wrong with lobbying – the problems come when people abuse the system to get advantages they shouldn't.

Lobbying is much like public relations, except that instead of the public, the lobbyists' target market is official bodies –

ministries, councils, political parties and individual MPs. Most of the work these people do is pretty straightforward – keeping their organisation or pressure group (or their clients) informed of relevant political decisions and setting up meetings with politicians to explain their position.

But most lobbyists are employed not just to write interesting summaries of the previous day's business in the House of Commons but because they have 'contacts' – the assumption being that if two lobbyists pitch up at a minister's door, the minister is more likely to let in the person they know (or at least the one representing an organisation they know). This is where the waters get a bit murkier, and where the important distinction between two types of lobbyist is relevant – those who work for a single organisation or pressure group, and those who work for a lobbying company and are then hired to lobby on behalf of a number of different organisations.

Generally, when people worry about lobbyists they mean the latter category. The democratic concern is that organisations which can afford expensive lobbyists are effectively buying access, and thereby getting an unfair opportunity to put their case to decision-makers. They are, but the million dollar question (although it's more like a multi-billion dollar question in this case) is what difference all that lobbying makes. And since no one really knows the answer to that question, there are constant demands for the whole process to be more open.

Lobbying: how to change a law

If a pressure group decides it's time for a change in the law, how do they go about lobbying for the change? Here are five tips for how to get things done (not necessarily in this order):

1. Make contact with as many MPs and peers as possible who might be sympathetic, or who are interested in the issue, to tell them about the need for the change.

2. Persuade an MP to table an early day motion (EDM) calling for the change – this will help gauge the level of parliamentary support.

3. Get like-minded people to contact their local MP, explaining about the issue and asking him or her to sign the EDM and contact the minister to press for the change.

4. Ask another MP or peer to ask questions of ministers, and see if an MP will submit a ten-minute rule Bill or, even better, a private member's Bill (see Chapter 4 for what these all do).

5. Contact the relevant minister – you'll almost certainly need their support to change the law, although sometimes they can introduce statutory instruments and even make decisions on their own authority. Ask for a meeting with the minister and take along a decent presentation. You can contact them directly, but if you don't have any luck that way ask your sympathetic MPs to write to them on your behalf.

6. Contact the media. The politicians will be even more likely to help if they can see that your campaign has momentum, and it will help bring your message to a wider audience.

What do pressure groups do?

Unsurprisingly, given their name, they put pressure on politicians to follow their agenda. 'Pressure group' is a bit of a catch-all phrase encompassing any group other than a political party which tries to put pressure on government – voluntary associations, trade associations and professional bodies, unions, charities and other NGOs (non-governmental organisations).

Many of these spend most of their time away from politics – some actively avoid it – but when they do enter the political fray they become a pressure group.

The most important thing pressure groups do is lobby. But they also campaign in other ways, often making a lot of effort to get media coverage, and spending time in influencing public opinion. Some, such as Greenpeace, Fathers4Justice or the Countryside Alliance, take direct action to try and make their point. This can involve demonstrating, protesting and civil disobedience.

The important thing about pressure groups is that they campaign on a narrow issue or set of issues – rural issues for the Countryside Alliance, for example; or the environment for Greenpeace. And the public seems to respond to these organisations. While the membership of political parties, and turnout in elections, has fallen in recent decades, the membership and amount of money donated to pressure groups has continued to rise. Many observers point to this public interest in pressure groups to argue that the public – and young people in particular – aren't apathetic about political issues, but about the political process and the way it's currently run.

Do politicians listen to public opinion, or just special interests?

Of course they listen to public opinion, but public opinion is often divided, and the strength of feeling is also important. Politicians also listen to their constituents (if they're elected), companies, charities, other governments and their own consciences when taking decisions. The balance between all these factors will vary depending on the decision. For example, on issues which are normally regarded as a matter of conscience, such as abortion or the death penalty, MPs' own views are often the most important. On other issues which are more party political, such as funding for education, health service reform or relations with Zimbabwe, they will be more influenced by people who have an interest in the subject ('stakeholders'), by their party policy and by public opinion.

A good example of where the 'political classes' regularly ignore public opinion is on the death penalty. Polls regularly show that there would be a great deal of public support for the re-introduction of the death penalty, yet it rarely arises in Westminster because there is so little parliamentary support for it. It's a clear example of politicians listening to their consciences rather than to public opinion.

8

Outside Westminster

While most people think of government and politicians as being based in London, in fact most are outside it. They are either based in local government (councils) around the country, or in the new 'devolved' institutions in Scotland, Wales and Northern Ireland. These various bodies provide many government services.

Since 1997 'devolution' – transferring power from central government to local units – has dramatically increased the powers of politicians outside London and has transformed the political scene. It has happened in Scotland with the creation of the Scottish Parliament, Wales and Northern Ireland with the establishment of their assemblies, and London with the setting up of the London Mayor and London Assembly (together known as the Greater London Authority, or GLA).

The different institutions have very different responsibilities, though. Scotland has a full parliament, which can pass laws on a pretty wide variety of subjects – although some (for example tax, defence and foreign policy) are reserved to Westminster. The assemblies in Wales and Northern Ireland have far fewer powers, while the GLA's powers are more limited still.

What do councils do?

Across England and Wales there are 21,000 councillors, who are elected to sit on 410 local authorities (or councils). They spend over £60 billion a year and employ more than two million people in providing many of the most important government services. Indeed many of the services which are mainly paid for by central government are actually delivered by local government, including housing, social services and education.

There are two different models of council – those which provide all the local authority services in a given area, and those where there are two tiers. It is not a hard and fast rule, but if you live in a city or large town, or if you live anywhere in Wales or Scotland, you are likely to have a single authority – either a 'unitary' council such as West Berkshire or a city council such as York. If you live outside a major city in England you are more likely to have two levels – for example, people who live in Alnwick, in the north-east of England, have both a district council (Alnwick District Council) and a county council (Northumberland County Council). London is different again: there are thirty-two borough councils plus the Corporation of London (the authority for the City of London), while the GLA has a co-ordinating role (see below).

In addition to these five types of local authority, many areas also have town and parish councils. These have few powers and are usually found in rural areas, although this is not always the case. Town and parish councils can provide community centres, arts and leisure facilities, parks and play areas, public conveniences and other services.

What services is my council responsible for?

County councils: Education, libraries, social services, trading standards, waste disposal, highways and transport, strategic land use planning.

District councils: Housing, parks, sports, arts and entertainment, land use planning permission, environmental health, waste collection and recycling, street cleaning, council tax collection, council tax and housing benefits, electoral registration and administration.

City councils and unitary councils: Because they are responsible for everything in their area, they combine the responsibilities of county and district councils.

How much power do they have?

In theory, the large number of services they deliver should mean they have a lot of power, and some of the larger councils do. But over the last thirty years both Labour and Conservative governments have tied councils' hands. By giving them more responsibilities and tying most of the extra funding to specific objectives, they have made it ever harder for the councils to decide for themselves how services should be delivered in their area.

Still, they do have some power, and recent local government reforms have aimed to make it easier to use that power to run the council well. They are now run by either a 'Cabinet' of super-councillors or a directly elected mayor (although councils have to hold a referendum if they want a directly elected mayor). But while these reforms have been far-reaching, these directly elected mayors remain far less powerful than big city mayors in the United States, for example.

Why is council tax always going up?

Councils currently get money from three sources:
- council tax – this tax, about 25 per cent of what the average council spends, is calculated on property values;
- local business rates – these account for another 21 per cent, also calculated on property values;
- government grant – the rest comes from the government.

Because of this, and the complicated way in which the government grant is calculated, a council has to raise its council tax bills by quite a lot to cover even quite modest increases in spending. And because central governments recently have been giving councils lots of new responsibilities but not always enough money to pay for them, those increases in spending have sometimes been far from modest – hence the rises.

The complicated government grant is intended to even out differences between councils – Guildford, in Surrey, for example, has much richer residents than Southwark, in London. But many critics of the council tax argue that it is very unfair, because it takes no account of income, only the value of a house (hence pensioners are particularly affected by this tax). Other critics complain that the complicated government grant system makes it difficult for voters to hold their local councils responsible when they get things wrong, and means they sometimes get the blame for decisions out of their control. Supporters argue that by leaving central government with the final say, they can stop councils wasting money.

Where does the mayor of London fit in?

That's difficult to answer, because while the mayor is directly elected and has a very high profile in London, the law which established the job put very firm limits on the mayor's formal powers. The first mayor, Ken Livingstone, has been highly skilled at using what powers he has to their very limits, making more of the position than many commentators thought likely.

In strategic planning in areas like land use, cultural policy, many environmental issues and economic development, for example, he has been able to shift policy to reflect his priorities. He is also responsible for setting the budgets of the Metropolitan Police, the fire brigade, Transport for London (which runs the Underground, the buses and the main roads) and the London Development Agency. The mayor will have a vital role to play in the run-up to the 2012 London Olympics.

But more than these, Livingstone has been skilled at using what the Americans call the 'bully pulpit' – the very high-profile nature of the job – to maximise his influence and persuade other people to do what he wants in these and other areas.

The London Assembly is supposed to keep a check on the mayor. In reality Assembly members have few powers and because political control in the Assembly has been divided between several groups they have struggled to restrain the mayor with the formal powers they do have – mainly amending the mayor's budget, launching investigations, summoning the mayor to answer questions and being consulted by him.

Will there be devolution to the regions?

There is a bit of confusion about regional government. The idea of elected regional assemblies in England has been dead since voters in the north-east decisively rejected an assembly there in 2004. However, the demise of regional assemblies does not mean the end of regional bodies – just the mechanism by which they are governed. Quangos such as the regional development agencies and the government offices for each region still exist, taking strategic decisions and trying to bring greater coherence to policy across their regions.

What are the 'devolved institutions'?

Devolution to Scotland, Wales and Northern Ireland has produced three bodies with very different powers and very different political complexions, but which share some of the basic structure.

Most important, because all three are subordinate to the UK Parliament in Westminster, many powers are still 'reserved' – held by the UK Parliament. These vary in each case, but generally cover policies which affect the whole of the United Kingdom, such as foreign and defence policy, immigration controls, national tax policy and a number of others.

The other key structural similarity is the management of relations between the devolved institutions – the parliament or assembly and its executive – and the UK Parliament and government. This is particularly important where two governments adopt different policies, in order to make sure that they at least work together, for example deciding what the arrangements were for English students at Scottish universities when Scotland abolished tuition fees.

What if they disagree with the UK government?

It's important that disputes between the devolved institutions and the government in London are resolved amicably, so there are two routes. Dispute resolution is mainly done directly with the Scottish, Welsh and Northern Ireland Offices in London. These offices are run by their own secretaries of state – members of the Cabinet – who used to be responsible for everything in those nations. Now the Secretaries of State for Wales and Scotland have far less to do – indeed so little that they combine it with running another government department. The Secretary of State for Northern Ireland remains rather busier, as a result of the oscillations of the peace process. Indeed at the time of writing the Northern Ireland Assembly and Executive have been suspended for as long as they have been active.

Any disagreements which can't be resolved directly between a devolved government and the secretary of state can be referred to the Joint Ministerial Committee, where representatives from all the institutions meet to discuss issues in which all four have an interest.

How does Scottish government work?

The Scottish Parliament and Executive were established in 1999. The Parliament has primary legislative powers, which means it can pass laws, on a broad, but limited, range of 'devolved' issues – see the box for what these are. The Executive is the government of Scotland for devolved matters, the equivalent of the UK Cabinet.

What's devolved and what's not in Scotland

Devolved
Justice
Education
Health
Community care
Enterprise
Local government
Finance
Environment and rural development
Social justice
Transport
Culture, tourism and sport

Reserved
Constitution and civil service
Foreign affairs and international development
Financial and economic matters
Defence and national security
Immigration and nationality
Drugs
Trade and industry
Energy regulation
Abortion, genetics, medicines
Broadcasting
Social security
Employment and equal opportunities

When the Scottish Parliament was set up in 1999, it re-established an institution which had been abolished in 1707. The distinct Scottish legal and educational systems, as well as the Church, had never been abolished, and still exist. In addition to passing laws in all the areas devolved to it, the Parliament can raise or lower the rate of income tax by 1 per cent – a penny in the pound – compared to the rate in the rest of Britain.

The Parliament has 129 members (Members of the Scottish Parliament or MSPs). They are elected in two different ways – seventy-three directly from constituencies, and the rest from lists of candidates drawn up by the parties, which make the Parliament more proportional. The system, called the 'additional member' system, is explained in more detail in the elections chapter.

The Scottish Parliament is different from the Westminster Parliament in two important ways – in the number of chambers (just one in Scotland), and in the power of the committees. In Scotland the committees both scrutinise proposed laws and keep a watching eye on the Scottish government departments. In this sense, they merge the powers of Westminster's standing committees and select committees, and are more like committees in the US Congress.

How is a law passed in Scotland?

Because there is only one chamber in the Scottish Parliament, it is more important that they get it right first time around. So, although the system is similar to the UK Parliament, there are some additional stages.

Stage 1   A Bill is proposed. It must be accompanied by a statement of the expected costs. The relevant committee discusses whether it should proceed to the next stage, and this is followed by a vote in the whole Parliament.

Stage 2   The Bill is considered in detail by one or more committees, with changes sometimes being made.

Stage 3	Further consideration by the full Parliament. Further amendments can be made and up to half the Bill can be sent back to the committee for further consideration.
Stage 4	Once the Bill is passed, it goes to the Queen for Royal Assent and becomes an Act of the Scottish Parliament.

MSPs have two other responsibilities – electing a Presiding Officer (much like the Speaker in the House of Commons) – and electing a First Minister (much like the Prime Minister). The Presiding Officer, although elected as a member of a political party, must be independent once chosen.

The First Minister is the most powerful political figure in Scotland. He is elected by the Parliament and must then appoint the other members of his government, known as the Scottish Executive. The First Minister is responsible for developing, presenting and implementing the policies of the Executive. He is also responsible for liaison with the Scottish Office in London and with other devolved bodies, where disagreements arise between them.

How does the Welsh Assembly work?

The National Assembly of Wales has far fewer powers than the Scottish Parliament, in large part because there was less demand for devolution in Wales than there was in Scotland. In fact in the referendum held in 1997, the turnout was just 50 per cent, and of those only 50.3 per cent voted 'yes' – a very small margin of victory. Structurally, though, devolution in Wales is similar to that in Scotland. It established two institutions: an Assembly, elected using PR, and an Assembly Cabinet (the government).

The crucial difference between Wales and Scotland is that in Wales, the Assembly is not able to pass primary legislation – that is, Acts of Parliament. Instead, it can only pass secondary legislation (in the form of statutory instruments known as 'Assembly Orders') on devolved matters, to modify the details of Acts. This power is not unimportant – many Acts leave lots of gaps to be filled in later through secondary legislation – but it is an important limitation on the Assembly. Many Welsh people and politicians from all parties have been frustrated by the limitations of their Assembly and argue that it should be granted powers equal to those of the Scottish Parliament.

The sixty-member Assembly is elected using the kind of PR seen in Scotland (the 'additional member' system). Forty members (known as AMs) are elected in constituencies while the other twenty come from party lists. Like the Scottish Parliament, the Assembly is chaired by a Presiding Officer. And again, although he or she must be an elected AM, the Presiding Officer must become politically impartial once elected.

The First Minister is the equivalent of a Welsh Prime Minister. He or she is responsible for appointing the Assembly Cabinet and has ultimate responsibility for all its policies. The Cabinet as a whole is elected by the Assembly, which means that the governing party must normally have a majority of seats.

What can the Welsh Assembly do?

The Welsh Assembly can pass secondary legislation in these areas:

- Agriculture and the environment
- Ancient monuments and historic buildings
- Culture, sport, tourism
- Economic development
- Health and health services
- Housing
- Industry

- Local government
- Roads and transport
- Social services
- Town and country planning
- The Welsh language

How did Northern Ireland get where it is today?

Northern Ireland is broadly split between two sides – unionists (who want to be part of the UK, and are generally Protestants) and nationalists (who want to be part of the Irish Republic, and are generally Catholics). These views tend to be held very passionately on both sides – the most passionate groups are known as 'loyalists' (on the unionist side) and 'republicans' (on the nationalist side).

Northern Ireland has a majority of unionists, and since it was formed in 1920 it has essentially been run by them. In the 1960s a movement amongst nationalists for equal rights in areas such as housing and education later became a political movement to join with the Irish Republic.

As both sides became more militant, tension rose between the communities and the violence which was spawned saw terrorist groups on both sides – the IRA (Irish Republican Army) and various loyalist groups – battling each other on the streets of Northern Ireland.

Little progress was made in stopping the violence until the early 1990s, when a peace process began, culminating in the signing of the Good Friday Agreement in 1998 and the efforts to implement it – both setting up the institutions and getting terrorists to decommission their weapons – since then.

Northern Ireland – a brief history

Like many long-running international conflicts around the world, history is a vitally important part of the conflict in Northern Ireland. Here are a few of the key events which have caused the legacy of such bitterness.

1170	The English invade Ireland.
1500s	Outsiders begin to settle on Irish lands, especially in Ulster.
1688–91	In 1688, the Catholic King James II of England is deposed and a Protestant, William of Orange, replaces him. James invades Ireland, but is defeated by William at the Battle of the Boyne in 1690 and a further defeat the following year ends the war. Much anti-Irish legislation is passed over the next thirty years.
1800s	Nationalist sentiment increases, including failed uprisings in 1848 and 1867; some political violence begins.
Late 1800s	Ireland has been part of the UK for a long time, and various 'Home Rule' Bills seeking to return power to Dublin are supported by Irish MPs and some Liberal MPs, but the Liberal Party splits and the Bills are rejected.
1916	Easter Rising in Dublin, when Irish Republican Brotherhood volunteers, later executed, fight for an Irish republic.
1919–23	War of Independence, in which the IRA fights Britain. In 1920, Ireland is divided between mainly Protestant Northern Ireland – part of the UK but with its own parliament; and a separate, overwhelmingly Catholic, Irish Free State, later the Irish Republic.

Late 1960s	Northern Ireland has been dominated by Protestant unionists since its inception, but in the 1960s a Catholic civil rights movement grows up to oppose discrimination against them. 'The Troubles' follow, as loyalist terrorists fight the IRA.
1972	Northern Ireland Parliament suspended to calm the violence.
1985	Anglo-Irish Agreement gives the Republic of Ireland influence over aspects of politics in Northern Ireland.
Early 1990s	Nationalists and republicans begin secret talks to try and start a peace process, resulting in elections to the Northern Ireland Forum in 1996 for peace talks.
1998	Good Friday Agreement signed, and approved in referendums in both Northern Ireland and the Irish Republic. Over the next seven years the peace process drags along, while the Assembly is set up and then suspended several times. Polarisation increases, with political power within both communities passing to political parties less inclined to reach agreement.
2005	IRA decommissions its weapons.

With that backdrop, how has devolution happened in Northern Ireland?

In one word, slowly. Movement towards devolution has been intimately related to movement in the peace process, always making it slow, and sometimes stopping it altogether.

The key milestone was the Belfast Agreement, signed on Good Friday 1998 (which is why it's also called the Good Friday Agreement) by the British and Irish governments and all the main political parties in Northern Ireland apart from the Democratic Unionist Party. All the parties involved compromised on important points to reach agreement, and many of the institutions, and their odd rules, are the product of those compromises.

The agreement's centrepiece was the setting up of a new devolved Northern Ireland Assembly and Executive, but bodies were also established to give the Irish Republic a greater role in how Northern Ireland should be run.

The agreement required paramilitary groups to scrap (or 'decommission') their weapons, terrorist prisoners to be released, and the Royal Ulster Constabulary (RUC) – the police force in Northern Ireland – to be reformed. The prisoner releases began shortly after it was signed, and in 2001 the RUC was re-named the Police Service of Northern Ireland to indicate its reform, but the weapons decommissioning took much longer and was not completed by the IRA until mid-2005.

So does the Northern Ireland Assembly work?

It often hasn't: devolution has been a victim of the difficulties which have plagued the peace process. On several occasions when the process has broken down, British Northern Ireland secretaries have simply suspended the Assembly and taken back its powers themselves. At the time of writing, it has been suspended for three years.

Even when it is running, its rules are the most complicated of the devolved institutions, because of the perceived need to involve all sides in the political process. So some issues are fully devolved, some which remain at Westminster might in future be devolved (reserved), while others never will be (excepted). See the box for what's what.

What's devolved and what's not – Northern Ireland

Devolved
Education and employment
Health
Transport
Arts and culture
Economic development and industry
Rural affairs and the environment
Local government and planning

Reserved
Postal services
Criminal law and the courts, policing
Import and export controls
National minimum wage
Financial services and markets
Competition policy
Units of measurement
Telecommunications
National Lottery
Abortion, human genetics, surrogacy and animal organ transplants
Data protection

Excepted
Elections
International relations
Defence and national security
Nuclear weapons, nuclear energy
Immigration and asylum

Taxes and duties
National insurance contributions
Regulation of sea fishing outside Northern Ireland

The Assembly has 108 members, known as MLAs (Members of the Legislative Assembly). They are elected using a form of PR (see Chapter 3 for an explanation).

The Assembly operates very much like the UK Parliament (except that it only has one chamber): laws are considered in a similar way and committees have similar responsibilities, although the Assembly only sits on Mondays and Tuesdays to give time for committee business the rest of the week.

The big differences are over the efforts to overcome Northern Ireland's bitter historical legacy and mistrust between the communities. To do so, Assembly and Executive rules require MLAs from both communities to work together. Not everyone is happy with these rules, and many unionists in particular are very critical of them.

The rules require MLAs to register their community affiliation – nationalist, unionist, or other – when first elected. When issues come to a vote, they can only pass if there is sufficient support in both communities. To that end proposals can pass in two different ways:

- simple majority, which requires more than 50 per cent of all votes and more than 50 per cent of both nationalist and unionist votes;
- weighted majority, which requires more than 60 per cent of all votes and more than 40 per cent of both nationalist and unionist votes.

The Northern Ireland Executive operates on the same principles. The First Minister and deputy First Minister stand for election jointly and must be elected by both sides of the Assembly. The other ten members of the Executive are appointed in proportion to their number of seats in the Assembly, meaning there is a broad representation in Northern Ireland's government (although there must be at least three nationalists and three unionists amongst the ten).

The Northern Ireland Assembly and Executive are based at Stormont Castle, six miles east of Belfast. In the same way that 'Westminster' is used as shorthand for the whole set-up in London, 'Stormont' is sometimes used to refer to devolved government in Northern Ireland.

Guide to the parties in Northern Ireland

Alliance	The Alliance is a non-sectarian party, linked to the Liberal Democrats.
DUP	The Democratic Unionist Party is run by Rev. Ian Paisley. The largest party in Northern Ireland, it strongly opposes the agreement and is the less flexible of the two main unionist parties on any kind of compromise with the nationalist and republican parties.
PUP	The small Progressive Unionist Party is linked to the loyalist UVF terror group, although it supports the agreement.
SDLP	The Social Democratic and Labour Party is a moderate nationalist party. Their MPs sit with the Labour Party in the House of Commons.
Sinn Fein	Sinn Fein is a Republican party, linked to the IRA. It has picked up a great deal of support since the agreement, supplanting the SDLP as the largest party on the nationalist side.
UKUP	The UK Unionist Party is a one-man band. Robert McCartney is the party's only MLA.
UUP	The Ulster Unionist Party used to be the largest unionist party, but lost support in recent years as unionist anger grew at concessions to nationalists and republicans.

What about co-operation with the Republic of Ireland?

One of the key components of the Good Friday Agreement was the creation of cross-border bodies. This was particularly important for nationalists, and resented by the unionists. There are several ways in which the Irish Republic now plays a political role in Northern Ireland.

The most important is the North–South Ministerial Council, which brings together ministers from the Northern Ireland Executive and the Irish Republic for consultations in areas such as agriculture, education, the environment, health, tourism and transport. Six special bodies were set up to implement any agreements reached by the council.

Two other bodies bring Northern Ireland and the Irish Republic together. First is the British–Irish Council or 'Council of the Isles', which is a pretty ineffective body designed to promote good relations. Every part of the British Isles, including the Channel Islands and Isle of Man, belongs to this.

More important is the British–Irish Intergovernmental Conference, which allows the two governments to have discussions on issues of joint interest. It also allows the Irish government to put forward proposals on issues relating to Northern Ireland which are controlled by Westminster.

Where does all this devolution leave England?

Many people think this is all a bit unfair on England. In fact part of the unfairness is known as the 'West Lothian question'. It is named after the constituency of the former Scottish MP Tam

115

Dalyell, an ardent opponent of devolution. When the first devolution schemes were proposed in the 1970s he asked about the fate of Scottish MPs after devolution. Today many others have begun to ask why Scottish MPs should be able to vote on matters which affect only England and Wales, when English and Welsh MPs have no similar rights for Scotland.

The question is particularly pertinent if on a vote about something only affecting England (English hospitals, say, or tuition fees at English universities) a majority of English MPs vote one way but lose the vote because of Scottish MPs voting the other way – on something which doesn't even affect their constituencies. Part of the way of dealing with this has been to reduce the number of Scottish MPs – in the 2005 general election it fell from 72 to 59.

But if in the future more powers are devolved to Wales and Northern Ireland, the question will be even more pressing. Some people propose that non-English MPs should be barred from voting on matters which only affect England; others argue that setting up an English Parliament would be the fairer solution, but at present there seems to be little momentum behind either proposal.

9

Beyond Britain

Britain might best be described as an unusually influential small country. This influence comes from three sources: our powerful economy, our history and our membership of the European Union.

Because Britain is a small country, there is sometimes a tendency to underplay our influence on the world stage. Yet Britain has the world's fourth largest economy – only the United States, Japan and Germany have larger economies (although China will soon overtake us, too). As it always has, this economic strength translates to political power: it makes Britain a member of groups such as the G8 (the world's largest economies), and pays for a relatively large and well-equipped military.

The historical legacy is also important. At the end of the nineteenth century Britain was the world's most powerful country, politically, economically and militarily. By the time the Second World War ended, Britain's best years had passed but Britain was still considered one of the 'Big Three' countries in the world (with the United States and the Soviet Union). While all three established the United Nations (UN), two other institutions – the World Bank and the International Monetary Fund (IMF) – were founded by Britain and the US alone, because the Soviet Union set itself apart.

The post-war legacy has also given us the Anglo-American 'special relationship'. The value – and indeed existence – of this relationship is much debated. However, there seems little doubt that at various points over the last sixty years it has been important in increasing British influence on the world stage.

The third source of Britain's influence in the world is our membership of the EU. The EU is vital in maximising our influence in trade and economic affairs, as well as influencing other European countries to behave in a certain way. But the issues surrounding European integration are extremely emotive. Answers to the questions in this chapter tend to give the views of both sides of the debate.

Most British Prime Ministers – particularly since the 1970s – have been keen to emphasise Britain's transatlantic role as a kind of bridge between the US and Europe, and Tony Blair is no different. His description of British influence is typical of how it has been seen by policy-makers for the last sixty years: 'Only a complete fool in today's world with its inter-dependence and globalisation would not rejoice at the fact that we are the key partner of the world's only superpower and we are a key player in the world's largest and most powerful political union.'

How does Britain use its influence?

In some really quite basic ways: British ministers and diplomats speak to their opposite numbers from other countries and try to persuade them to do what we want. Sometimes this involves close, long-term relationships (as with the US or other EU countries) and on other occasions more fleeting ones.

Foreign Office diplomats spend much of their time tending to relationships with countries all over the world so that crises don't happen, and if they do they can be resolved more easily. During the Falklands War, for example, the United States and Chile both played vital roles in Britain's victory, which they were prepared to do largely because of long-standing and well-tended relationships. In contrast the run-up to the Iraq war is regarded as a diplomatic failure, because British ministers and diplomats failed to persuade other countries to back the British position.

One important way in which diplomacy operates is through international agreements – either bilaterally (between two countries) or multilaterally (between more than two countries). Important multilateral agreements provide frameworks within which countries operate their own national policies for all sorts of issues. Contentious issues at present include the agreement for an International Criminal Court and the Kyoto protocol on climate change.

Before 'summits' – when national leaders get together to reach these sorts of major agreement – diplomats work frantically to prepare the groundwork. They will identify areas for common agreement and seek to narrow the gaps dividing the sides. When the political leaders arrive, only the most difficult decisions are left to be resolved. This is done through a process of bargaining.

Where does the EU fit in?

The European Union (EU) is a political and economic union of twenty-five countries. The economic ties are very strong – it originally concentrated on economic co-operation – and in recent years its political ties have become stronger.

Britain has been a member since 1973, although the EU has existed in a recognisable form since 1957. Since then, Britain's membership of the EU has affected us more than that of any other international organisation. This is because it has altered the nature of Britain's relationships with other European countries by making them part of the daily domestic political round. Many of the laws now passed in Britain originate in Europe, and many of our most important economic and political relationships operate through the prism of the EU.

But Britain's relationship with the EU (and sometimes even our membership of it) has been amongst the most divisive political issues of the last fifty years. It stirs real passions (albeit amongst a relatively small group of people) but the debate is not always well informed, and some of the important issues are frequently misunderstood. The EU's critics are often called 'Eurosceptics', while pro-Europeans are sometimes known as 'Europhiles'.

How does the EU affect Britain?

In an increasing number of ways. Most directly, a substantial proportion of British legislation – no one knows exactly how much, although some have suggested as much as 50 per cent – now originates in the EU. This has all sorts of implications for British politics.

For government ministers, negotiating with other European governments and with the European Commission is now part of their daily routine. These meetings and negotiations are regular and are handled by the departments themselves, rather than by diplomats at the Foreign Office. And the subjects covered are increasingly wide – everything from climate change to whether the government could give financial support to MG Rover.

For Parliament, it means that so many laws come from Europe (what's known as 'secondary' – or 'delegated' – legislation) that there isn't time to scrutinise them properly in the UK. Many Eurosceptics say that it's hard for an individual or business to know how to influence a law which will affect them, and they call this part of the EU's 'democratic deficit'.

What have the Europeans ever done for us?

Asking this question is a bit like the Judean People's Front, in Monty Python's *Life of Brian*, asking, 'What have the Romans ever done for us?' . . . Well, they've provided half a century of peace and prosperity, free trade, environmental protection and social programmes. Yes, but apart from *that*, what have the Europeans ever done for us?

Some of these things might have happened without European integration. Many people, for example, argue that the post-war peace has been more the result of NATO and the American nuclear umbrella. But others have unquestionably contributed to our quality of life. Generally, these benefits fall into two categories – internal and external.

Internal benefits include free trade and economic integration, and working more closely together on a wide range of policies (for example to improve cross-border policing). Sometimes some of the rules and regulations passed to make the single market work seem absurd, but many are necessary so that companies from all European countries can compete fairly across Europe.

External co-operation is based on the assumption that EU members have more power together than individually. This can be true for everything from co-ordinating relief efforts in developing countries to negotiating trade agreements or environmental treaties with the United States. This sometimes produces bizarre results – as when an agreement signed with China to limit Chinese textile exports to the EU resulted in millions of garments being held in warehouses across Europe – the so-called 'bra wars'.

How is the EU organised?

The EU is unique – there isn't anything like it anywhere else in the world – but it is organised a bit like a country: it has its own parliament; government of sorts, with a president and civil service departments; a central bank with its own currency; and a set of courts to enforce the laws.

The European Commission is the EU's permanent bureaucracy. Its role is to propose new laws and make sure they are implemented properly, and many people regard it as the most important EU institution. Its critics say it combines major power with a worrying lack of accountability, and argue that it frequently presses for new laws (see box) without any proper democratic oversight. They are particularly concerned that many decisions are taken in secret. The Commission is run by a President and twenty-four Commissioners, who are selected by European governments and approved by the Parliament.

The two other crucial EU institutions – which are like two houses of parliament – are the European Parliament and the Council of Ministers. The European Parliament, which contains elected members from every EU country, is like the House of Commons. With the Council, it can decide on laws and the EU's budget, but it can't initiate laws and doesn't have any role in setting taxes.

The Council of Ministers, officially named the Council of the European Union, is more like a senate: it is the main EU decision-making body. Each national government is represented on the Council – but the agenda dictates which minister represents the government. For example, if it's environment on the agenda, it will be all the environment ministers from all member states. These ministers meet regularly to discuss and agree a programme of action in their area. They have the power to veto new proposals in some important areas (for example tax).

The European Council is like a super-committee of the

Council of Ministers. Its members are the heads of government or heads of state of each EU country. Its role is more strategic – it meets every three months to agree the EU's objectives, set the budget and resolve the thorny problems which couldn't be dealt with elsewhere.

How is an EU law passed?

1. The Commission proposes a new law.
2. The European Parliament considers and votes on it.
3. The European Council or Council of Ministers considers and votes on it. In some important areas, for example tax, countries have a 'national veto'; in other areas a certain proportion of countries needs to vote for a proposal (because each country's vote is weighted according to its population, this is known as 'qualified majority voting').
4. The Parliament and Council have another look, after which it becomes law.
5. Each member state must implement the new law (in Britain this is normally through secondary legislation), while the Commission monitors whether they've done it properly.

What do MEPs do?

MEPs (members of the European Parliament) are directly elected from each European country. Countries have different numbers of MEPs depending on the size of their population. In the UK, which has seventy-eight MEPs, they are elected from regional party lists. Each British party belongs to a European 'group' – so Labour MEPs, for example, are members of the Group of European Socialists. On some crucial issues MEPs vote by country, and not by what their European group thinks. Some Europhile critics of this arrangement argue that MEPs should stop voting by country and instead vote by European political group; their Eurosceptic opponents say MEPs should definitely vote to support the national interest.

MEPs spend their time between two cities. The European Parliament's committees are based in Brussels, which is where MEPs spend most of their time. But once a month, they all move to Strasbourg for a week to meet in plenary session. Bizarrely, the parliamentary secretariat is in another city again, Luxembourg. This all came about because of compromises between the various countries which founded the EU.

What do the different European courts do?

This is one of the most confusing parts of the European Union. Because there are three European courts, people often mix them up. They are:

- The European Court of Justice. Based in Luxembourg, this is the EU's court. It settles arguments between countries and deals with cases brought against EU institutions.
- The European Court of Auditors. It isn't really a court at all, being more like a financial watchdog, making sure the EU is spending its money properly.
- The European Court of Human Rights. This isn't actually part of the EU – it was set up to judge cases brought under the European Convention on Human Rights (in Britain covered by the Human Rights Act). The rulings of this court come above those of the courts in any individual country.

How did we get into the EU?

How we got into and stayed in the European Union was a real back-and-forth over more than thirty years:

No	In 1951 six European countries (Belgium, France, Italy, Luxembourg, the Netherlands and West Germany) set up the European Coal and Steel Community, the forerunner of a European free trade area – the European Economic Community (or EEC). Britain saw itself as a 'Great Power' and decided not to join.
Yes	Amid increasing awareness of its relative decline, Britain decided it needed to join after all. The first application was made in 1961 under the Conservatives, and the second in 1967 under Labour. Both were vetoed by France. Our third application was accepted and Britain became a member in 1973, at the same time as Ireland and Denmark.
Maybe	In 1974 the new (Labour) government renegotiated Britain's membership and then held a referendum (Britain's first) on whether to stay in the EEC. Two-thirds of people voted to stay in.

Why don't we join the euro?

Britain stayed clear of early moves to turn the EEC from a free trade area towards a closer economic union. Nevertheless, Britain did eventually join the Exchange Rate Mechanism, designed to bring greater stability to international currency markets and get the European currencies balanced before an eventual single currency.

However, Britain was a member for only two years, from

1990 to 1992, before pressure from the currency markets forced it out. 'Black Wednesday', as it was called, put an end to most British governments' aspirations to join European monetary union. And opinion polls suggest there is continued public opposition to it (although many Europhiles complain this is more because of negative media coverage – people would be more in favour if the media were more balanced, they argue).

Still, there are three main areas of argument about joining the euro:

- Economic grounds. Europhiles say it would create a more stable (and lower) exchange rate, make it easier for British companies to export to our main markets – in Europe – and create jobs. Eurosceptics point to how some countries (particularly France and Germany) routinely flout the rules which are supposed to keep the euro stable. They argue that this would damage Britain's economy.

- Sovereignty. Eurosceptics say handing control of exchange rates to the European Central Bank would be wrong: they say it would be the first step on the road to a single European state.

- Politics. Many Europhiles argue that joining the euro would be a valuable political gesture which would give Britain greater influence on many other issues. Eurosceptics tend to dismiss this argument, arguing that there is no guarantee of the benefits, while the dangers are clear.

How much does the EU cost us, and what does it spend our money on?

Britain pays about £12 billion to the EU each year. We get about £4 billion from various budgets, plus a 'rebate' of £3.7 billion – intended to compensate Britain for what would otherwise be a large gap between what we put in and what we receive. Because of the way the British economy is structured, without the rebate we would pay more in and get less out than most other European countries. As it is, our 'net' contribution is still £4.3 billion. In 2005 a new budget deal set a higher level for the EU budget and reduced the rate by which the UK rebate will rise.

Politicians from all British parties tend to be extremely critical of how the EU spends its money. The Common Agricultural Policy (CAP) is particularly widely reviled, and is often regarded in Britain as wasteful, corrupt and damaging to the developing world. However, farmers in the parts of Europe which depend on the support would never accept the abolition of the CAP. French farmers, in particular, take this view but they are certainly not alone.

The EU gets its money from its members. It has a total budget of €111 billion, about £76 billion (a similar budget to the NHS). It spends the vast majority of this on two areas: farming (€47bn in 2004) and supporting Europe's poorer regions (€41bn in 2004). The rest (about €12bn) is spent on administration and all its other policies – international development, the environment, cultural activities and so on.

Why did it change from the EEC to the EU?

When Britain joined, in 1973, the organisation was called the European Economic Community (EEC). The EEC was basically a glorified free trade area. It changed its name to the European Community in 1991 and became the European Union in 1993, after the Maastricht treaty.

This new name reflected the increasingly political nature of the EU. But EU members are split on whether to proceed with closer political union (becoming a federation like the United States) and, if so, how far or fast.

No British government of the last thirty years has shown any great enthusiasm for the more close-knit aspects of political union, no doubt at least in part because British public opinion remains so opposed to it. In the last few years one political party, the United Kingdom Independence Party, has emerged which argues that Britain should pull out of the EU altogether.

Could we leave the EU?

Yes we could, although in Britain most political parties don't want to: they argue that the consequences would be extremely serious. Even many Eurosceptics make a point of saying they don't believe it would be in Britain's interests to pull out of the EU – they want to make it a looser association with fewer rules and greater freedom for manoeuvre.

Those who want to pull out believe it would produce huge benefits under three main headings:

- finance – we would save £4.3 billion;
- economy – we could trade more easily with the rest of the world because we could abolish the high tariff barriers protecting the European market;
- sovereignty – we would recover control over our own affairs, and could abolish lots of silly and unnecessary European rules and regulations, which would help the economy and society.

As ever, opposing them are many others who argue that leaving the EU would be bad for Britain. They say we would lose out in four areas:

- economy – having less direct access to European markets would mean less foreign investment in Britain and fewer British jobs;

- sovereignty – in order to trade with Europe we would still have to abide by European rules but we'd no longer have a say in making them;
- lost influence – the EU is a powerful trading bloc and Britain would lose influence at international trade negotiations if it pulled out;
- reduced co-operation – Britain would lose the co-operation which it gets in important areas such as cross-border crime and development assistance.

Which countries are members of the EU (in 2006)?

The EU currently has twenty-five members:

Austria	Lithuania
Belgium	Luxembourg
Cyprus	Malta
Czech Republic	Netherlands
Denmark	Poland
Estonia	Portugal
Finland	Republic of Ireland
France	Slovakia
Germany	Slovenia
Greece	Spain
Hungary	Sweden
Italy	United Kingdom
Latvia	

Two more countries, Bulgaria and Romania, are set to join on 1 January 2007, and membership negotiations are being held with Croatia and Turkey.

What role does Britain play at the UN?

The United Nations is rather like an extended family of octopuses, with hundreds of limbs covering everything from health (WHO) and education (UNESCO) to refugees (UNHCR). But the three key political bodies are the UN General Assembly, a kind of parliament where every member is represented; the United Nations Organization (UNO), its secretariat or civil service; and the Security Council (UNSC), which is like an executive committee for taking policy decisions on international affairs.

The UN was established in 1945 in an effort to avoid the international conflicts which led to the Second World War. Its structures reflect the distribution of power in the world at that time – the three key countries were the United States, the Soviet Union and Britain.

Britain largely relies on its position on the UNSC for its influence. Britain is one of only five permanent members (known as the 'P5' – the others are the United States, Russia, China and France), with nine others elected from the General Assembly to serve two-year terms. The P5, in addition to being permanent, can also veto any proposed UNSC motion, even if it would otherwise have had a majority.

The reason all this matters is that Security Council resolutions count as international law – all 191 UN members have to obey them.

The other way in which Britain can influence world affairs through the UN is by providing material support for UN resolutions – money or troops. Because Britain is a wealthy country with a relatively large and well-equipped army and aid budget, this gives us more influence than countries without such benefits.

Do we still need NATO?

NATO is the North Atlantic Treaty Organisation. Established in 1948, it established a defence relationship between the United States, Canada and the democratic countries of western Europe against the threat posed by the Soviet Union and the Warsaw Pact countries.

Critics complain that since the Soviet Union collapsed and the Cold War ended more than a decade ago, NATO is increasingly redundant. Its remit has certainly broadened – its membership has expanded to twenty-six countries and since the end of the Cold War has operated in Bosnia, Kosovo and Afghanistan. Although there are moves afoot to create some European defence bodies, they don't come anywhere close to being a European army. So for the time being, at least, NATO remains our most important international defence agreement: Britain is an important member because of our well-equipped, well-trained and relatively large armed forces.

Which countries are members of NATO?

Belgium	Lithuania
Bulgaria	Luxembourg
Canada	Netherlands
Czech Republic	Norway
Denmark	Poland
Estonia	Portugal
France	Romania
Germany	Slovakia
Greece	Slovenia
Hungary	Spain
Iceland	Turkey
Italy	United Kingdom
Latvia	United States

What does the Commonwealth do, other than organise games every so often?

It depends on your point of view. Sceptics say that it is an outdated institution which means little; its supporters argue that this less formal coalition of very different countries with a shared history makes a real contribution to improved global understanding.

The Commonwealth's strengths are its history and diversity – it grew out of the 'British Commonwealth' of countries which once made up the British Empire. When the empire broke up over the course of the twentieth century, many were keen to retain the shared language, culture and history, but without the imperial overtones. As such, the Commonwealth is huge (1.8 billion people across five continents) and uniquely diverse in bringing together developed world countries such as Britain and Australia, somewhat developed countries such as South Africa and developing countries across Africa and Asia. Of course, bringing them together is all very well, but in recent crises in Pakistan and Zimbabwe, critics have complained that the Commonwealth has been unable to effect its will.

The Queen remains head of the Commonwealth, and is still the head of state of sixteen of its fifty-three members – including, for example, Australia and Canada. It is apparently one of the political parts of her job she enjoys most.

What do the IMF, the World Bank and the WTO do?

These three institutions were established at the end of the Second World War to shape the post-war world so as to bring stability and a degree of openness to international trade and avoid the economic protectionism which preceded the war. Although the WTO (World Trade Organization) only came into existence in 1995, its predecessor, GATT (the General Agreement on Tariffs and Trade), was, with the International Monetary Fund (IMF) and the World Bank, founded at the end of the Second World War.

Although they are often spoken about together, particularly by their critics, they have different functions. The World Bank lends money for development projects, the IMF lends money to stabilise currencies and whole economies, while the WTO works to create freer international trade.

Britain played a crucial role in the creation of each institution, and our economic power means we remain an important member. Since the 1970s, when Britain had to ask the IMF for a loan to overcome our own economic difficulties, our economy has strengthened and in recent years the British government has used its membership of the IMF and World Bank to push for international debt relief.

And the G8?

The G8 is like a rich men's club – the richest seven countries in the world (Canada, France, Italy, Germany, Japan, the UK and the US) plus Russia, added largely to soothe its hurt feelings about no longer being a superpower. Normally, the G8 cycle and its schedule of meetings are just another part of the international diplomatic calendar, with very little to show at the end. However, that isn't always the case, as the British government showed in 2005 when it used its G8 presidency to push for a programme of assistance to Africa.

10

Politics and the law

Even before the 9/11 attacks in New York and Washington, but particularly since, a huge debate has been raging about what powers the government needs to deal with terrorism. To the squeal of human rights lawyers, the police have demanded, and Parliament has tended to grant them, ever greater powers to help them tackle the terrorist threat. The balance between individual liberty and state power, even between the rights and responsibilities of individuals towards one another, has been at the forefront of public debate.

Every so often, Parliament is asked to look again at those powers, decides anew where that balance should lie, and passes a new law. But the debate doesn't end there. Instead, it merely moves to a different world, one which is populated by the people using the new powers – police officers, spies and occasionally members of the armed forces – and those who will interpret them and decide whether they are legal – the lawyers and judges. It is these worlds, of implementation and of judicial interpretation, which are covered in this chapter. However, it doesn't cover Scotland, which has had its own legal system since the medieval era, or Northern Ireland, which also has a slightly different legal system.

Some useful legal terms

Solicitor: Lawyer who can advise clients but has only a limited right to argue cases in court. About 90 per cent of lawyers are solicitors.

Barrister: Lawyer who argues cases in court. Can be retained via a solicitor or other select professionals, e.g. accountants.

QC: Queen's Counsel, a senior barrister.

Civil law: Law dealing with normal dealings between people, including family law, business law and property law.

Criminal law: Law involving violence, injury, theft and fraud.

What is the judicial system?

The judicial system is the court system, one of the three branches of British government. It is independent of government, an independent judiciary being a very important principle in a democracy where everyone is equal in the eyes of the law.

The judiciary used to be regarded as the least powerful branch of government, but increasingly it is in the courts where some of the most profound disagreements in British politics are argued out. This has come about in part because of changes to the constitution which empower judges to challenge government decisions. However, it is mainly because in Britain previous legal judgments – known as 'precedents' – themselves form a part of the law, and so carry a great deal of weight.

Different types of court

Magistrates' courts: These courts deal with more than 90 per cent of criminal cases. They are run by magistrates (also known as Justices of the Peace, or JPs), who are part time and often have other jobs.

County courts: Deal with most basic civil cases.

Crown courts: Deal with all criminal cases not dealt with in magistrates' courts. They are organised in different tiers to deal with crimes of different severity. The Old Bailey in London, officially called the Central Criminal Court, is the most famous crown court in the country, and the most serious crimes are often tried there.

High Court: This court has three divisions, although most of the casework for all three is civil law: the Family Division; the Chancery Division, which deals with most business and property law; and the Queen's Bench Division, which deals with other civil law, for example libel, breach of contract and torts ('civil wrongs' such as car accidents).

Court of Appeal: The court's two divisions deal with criminal and civil law appeals respectively.

House of Lords/Supreme Court: The House of Lords' legal role will soon be transferred to a new Supreme Court. This is the highest court in the land, where both branches of law end.

European courts: Few cases reach these courts, but the European Court of Human Rights can overrule British interpretations of the Human Rights Act and the European Court of Justice can declare British laws incompatible with EU treaties, effectively superseding British courts.

Who are the Law Lords?

The Law Lords are formally known as 'Lords of Appeal in Ordinary'. They are the country's most senior judges, and are the equivalent of other countries' Supreme Court justices. The Law Lords have traditionally sat as the Appellate Committee of the House of Lords, Britain's highest court. They hear cases in their own room but deliver judgments in the main House of Lords chamber – ordinary members of the House of Lords haven't heard legal cases for more than 100 years.

The same Law Lords also sit as the Judicial Committee of the Privy Council, which is the final court of appeal for several Commonwealth countries and also hears cases about devolution within the UK – i.e. where the Westminster Parliament and one of the devolved institutions can't agree who has jurisdiction over a particular subject.

In 2005, however, the Constitutional Reform Act was passed, which will turn the House of Lords Appellate Committee into a new, and separate, Supreme Court. This will abolish the odd situation whereby our highest court is formally part of Parliament. The Lord Chancellor will be replaced as head of the judiciary by the Lord Chief Justice.

Changing the law: the Human Rights Act

The Human Rights Act (HRA), passed in 1998, is one of the furthest-reaching and most controversial pieces of legislation in many years. It put into British law the European Convention on Human Rights (ECHR), a document drafted in 1950 to protect fundamental freedoms for European countries. While many of the rights in the ECHR had long existed in British law it introduced others, such as respect for private and family life, for the first time.

The HRA covers all public authorities. Furthermore, all other pieces of legislation must comply with it. When introducing new Bills, for example, the government now has to give a specific declaration that it complies with the HRA. The government can only introduce something prohibited by the HRA, known as 'derogation', in times of emergency.

What powers do judges have?

Every judge is responsible for the trial in their courtroom. They are responsible for its management, for clarifying points of law for the jury (if there is one) and, if there is a guilty verdict for a criminal offence, for sentencing the offender. This is what happens in most trials, which are either criminal cases where the only question is the guilt or innocence of the person on trial or civil cases needing some kind of resolution.

Some cases – generally those which reach the Court of Appeal and the House of Lords – have wider political significance, however, often being used to test the judges' interpretation of a new law, for example. The judges in charge of these cases have greater political influence because the lower courts must follow the precedents they set. Judicial review – where judges supervise how public officials and public bodies do their jobs – is another important procedure for holding the government to account.

The changes under the HRA have been the furthest-reaching, however. If they find that laws are in breach of the HRA, judges have two options:

- If the law is primary legislation (i.e. an Act of Parliament), they can issue a 'declaration of incompatibility', which governments don't have to obey but normally want to.
- If the law is secondary legislation (such as a statutory instrument), judges can strike it down. Since this forms the bulk of legislation, their power is substantial.

Constitutional developments in recent years, together with the creation of the Supreme Court, may also result in a de facto constitutional court, which will play an important role in deciding constitutional cases.

How are judges appointed?

The system for judicial appointments has always been shrouded in secrecy. Judges were appointed by the Lord Chancellor after taking 'soundings' within the profession. Many people regarded that system as unacceptably secretive, particularly for Law Lords and other judges who have a more political role. As a result, the system is due to be overhauled and a new Judicial Appointments Commission will take over responsibility of this area.

Who is the Lord Chancellor?

The Lord Chancellorship is one of the ancient offices of state, dating back to at least the eleventh century, and until recently one of the most powerful. The Lord Chancellor was unique in being a member of all three branches of government – the executive (as a Cabinet minister), the judiciary (as the head of the judiciary) and the legislature (as a member of, and chairing debates in, the House of Lords).

Much of that, however, is about to change. While some of the ancient and ceremonial aspects of the role will continue, two crucial roles will disappear, leaving the Lord Chancellor more like a normal Cabinet minister – the Secretary of State for Constitutional Affairs, as the job has also been known since 2003. The two jobs which disappear are:

- head of the judiciary, which the Lord Chief Justice will take over;
- chairing debates in the House of Lords, as the second chamber will elect its own speaker.

Who decides what sentences to give?

The trial judge, although people can appeal against their sentences. Judges sentence offenders according to sentencing guidelines, which take into account all sorts of factors – from how best to protect the public, reduce crime and punish offenders, to how to rehabilitate the offenders. Other factors, such as whether offenders apologise or show remorse, whether they plead innocent or guilty, and their personal circumstances, also play a role in the sentencing.

Most crimes are relatively minor, which helps to explain why less than 10 per cent of convictions result in a prison sentence; the vast majority of offenders are fined instead. Of the offenders sent to prison, few serve the full length of their sentence: most are eligible for early supervised release (known as parole).

Some crimes carry a minimum sentence (for example, trafficking Class A drugs carries a minimum seven-year sentence). The rules are strictest for murder, which carries a minimum term of a life sentence. A life sentence rarely means imprisonment for life, however. Instead, the judge sets a 'tariff', the minimum length of time the murderer must serve before being considered for release. The Home Secretary used to have this power, but it was removed as a result of the Human Rights Act.

What does the Attorney General do?

His main job is as the government's lawyer. He (there has never yet been a female Attorney General) provides the government with legal advice and represents the government in court if necessary.

However, 'the Attorney' (as he's known in official shorthand) is also a member of the government and usually a member of the

Cabinet. These roles merge in his ministerial responsibilities – he oversees the Director of Public Prosecutions, the head of the Crown Prosecution Service (see box).

The Attorney General and Solicitor General (the government's second law officer) have both traditionally been senior barristers, although in recent years the Solicitor General has sometimes been a solicitor.

Who prosecutes criminals?

The Crown Prosecution Service (CPS) is responsible for all criminal prosecutions in England and Wales; in Scotland this is handled by a body called the Crown Office and Procurator Fiscal Service.

The police investigate criminal cases and then pass a file of evidence to the CPS, which decides whether to prosecute. Not all police investigations result in a prosecution: in every case the CPS has two tests when deciding whether to proceed with a prosecution:

- the evidential test: whether the available evidence gives them a good chance of getting a conviction;
- the public interest test: for example, would prosecuting a very complicated case give good value for money? Would a prosecution badly affect the victim's mental or physical health?

The CPS uses the same tests when deciding whether to prosecute cases handed to it by other investigating bodies, such as the Health and Safety Executive.

For cases of major fraud, the Serious Fraud Office is normally the prosecuting authority, and not the CPS.

Why do we have legal aid?

Legal aid is the money given to people who otherwise couldn't afford legal representation. Since lawyers are expensive, it is a vital mechanism in ensuring equality before the law in practice, and not just in principle. Legal aid is a pretty controversial subject on occasion, normally when newspapers get incensed at somebody being awarded aid for an unworthy case, but in general the guidelines are clear and the principle widely accepted.

Why are civil liberties important?

Civil liberties are protections from the power of governments. Originally, they were a way of escaping the king's oppression: in the Magna Carta in 1215 King John set out certain rights for the nobles. Those rights gradually worked their way down to every British person and are an important part of the British liberal democratic tradition.

Civil liberties have become more widespread almost continuously since then, and since the Human Rights Act was passed in 1998 a tranche of new rights have appeared in British law. However, the balance between individual rights and responsibilities, and between individual rights and the power of the state, is a complicated one to get right. Often, the issues aren't even framed in terms of civil liberties but there are often such implications. Consider these examples:

- wearing a motorbike helmet – balancing motorcyclists' right to ride with the wind in their hair against the public need to increase safety;
- foxhunting – balancing the right of a minority to continue their pastime against the right of the majority to outlaw something many consider to be unacceptable;

- smoking – balancing people's right to smoke in public places and damage their own health against the right of the majority to breathe clean air and reduce smokers' healthcare costs.

Some of these – like bike helmets and smoking – are more about the government forcing people to do what is good for them. But in other cases, for example most anti-terrorist legislation, an individual's civil liberty may be removed with no balancing individual benefit – instead the benefit is to society as a whole. Still, there is often stiff opposition to such legislation, particularly when it removes fundamental or long-held rights. The Bills are often challenged in court, where judges have the tricky task of balancing civil liberties against the government's legitimate need to ensure the safety of the nation.

Similar questions arise when the stakes are not so high on either side – for example in criminal justice legislation. One reason the government's introduction of ASBOs (anti-social behaviour orders) has been so controversial is because of the way they remove an individual's civil liberties; balanced against that is the right of the wider community not to have their lives disrupted by one individual's anti-social behaviour.

Who is in charge of the police?

Each police force has three different sets of management, with responsibility split between the chief constable of each force, the local police authority and the Home Office.

The chief constable is responsible for running the police force; the police authority, a quango composed of local councillors and magistrates, sets the budget, decides the strategic priorities and monitors police performance; the Home Office provides part of the funding and sets targets and minimum standards. The real power is shared by the chief constable and the Home Office.

Complicating matters further is the way policing is structured across the country. There is no national police force; instead it is divided into a number of different constabularies (at the time of writing the forty-three forces are being merged to create a smaller number of new forces). The funding reflects this – like many services delivered locally, money comes both from local taxation and from a central government grant. Yet the mechanism for getting local accountability, the police authority system, has relatively little influence in the process.

Are the police racist?

Probably no more and no less than any other organisation – after all, any organisation will contain individuals with unpleasant views. The obvious difference is that if a police officer acts on those unpleasant views, the result is more serious than if many other people did so.

In recent years this whole issue has become very high profile – particularly since the police were accused of being 'institutionally racist'. The phrase draws a distinction between individual bigotry and systemic problems which unintentionally produce racist outcomes. It was used in the report of the 1999 Macpherson inquiry, set up after the bungled Metropolitan Police investigation into the racist murder of black teenager Stephen Lawrence. They concluded that the police needed to modify their procedures to prevent further such failures.

The issue of race will remain a complicated one in policing Britain's multi-racial society. The balance between vigorous and effective policing on the one hand and appearing to victimise certain ethnic groups on the other can sometimes be a fine one.

In the 1980s and 1990s, the police faced this challenge with the black community; in the noughties it is a particular challenge with the Asian community.

What do the intelligence agencies do?

The intelligence agencies are responsible for getting hold of secret information ('intelligence') about enemies and potential enemies. Some of this involves spying of the James Bond variety, although a lot of it consists of the more mundane collecting of information. Britain has a number of different agencies doing this, with different responsibilities. The resulting intelligence is used by ministers and officials to decide policy in all sorts of areas.

The agencies involved are:

Security Service (MI5): Responsible for spying and intelligence gathering within the UK, particularly to protect the country against terrorism.

Secret Intelligence Service (SIS or MI6): Responsible for spying and intelligence gathering overseas. This is where James Bond worked.

Government Communications Headquarters (GCHQ): Intercepts and decodes communications from around the world.

Defence Intelligence Staff (DIS): The intelligence body within the Ministry of Defence, which focuses on military intelligence.

Joint Intelligence Committee (JIC): Sits at the heart of the government's intelligence machinery. It advises on priorities for intelligence collection and draws together intelligence from all the other agencies to provide assessments which go to ministers and senior officials.

Special Branch: Part of the Metropolitan Police, responsible for collecting intelligence and conducting operations against political extremists and terrorists.

National Criminal Intelligence Service (NCIS): Provides police forces with intelligence support on serious and organised crime, not terrorism.

Who controls the armed forces?

The three armed services – army, navy and air force – are answerable to the Ministry of Defence. The chain of command goes through the individual service chiefs to the Chief of the General Staff and the Secretary of State for Defence, and beyond them to the Cabinet and the Prime Minister.

The armed services can't initiate action on their own, nor can they refuse to take action if told to do so; this is what is meant by civilian control of the military. The only situation in which a military commander might refuse to serve was if he believed it was illegal to do so, thereby placing his troops in legal jeopardy. This is why military commanders were so insistent on receiving a clear legal opinion prior to the war in Iraq.

During a war, government control tends to be tightly centralised into a 'war Cabinet' – an inner core of ministers with political and departmental responsibility for all aspects of the war. In recent conflicts, there have been early morning meetings in the 'Cobra' room (which, rather disappointingly, just stands for 'Cabinet Office Briefing Room A'), underneath the Cabinet Office. This is the same room from which the government response to terrorist attacks and other emergencies is co-ordinated.

11

Economy

The British economy is the world's fourth largest, after those of the United States, Japan and Germany (although it is shortly to be pushed into fifth place by China). This relative strength is a quite recent development – for most of the post-war period Britain's economy grew much more slowly than our major competitors, and by the end of the 1970s Britain was in a poor position.

The dramatic turnaround in our economic performance since then has had major political implications. Tax revenue has increased even as tax rates have fallen, and public spending has grown steadily. Management of the economy has remained a central political issue but expectations of good economic performance and high standards of living have replaced 'managing decline' in political discourse.

Some common economic terms	
GDP	Gross domestic product, all economic activity within a country
GNP	Gross national product, all economic activity which belongs to a country (so the earnings of a multinational company based in Britain would be included in the British GNP)
Fiscal policy	Taxation and spending policy
Inflation	Prices rising
Monetary policy	Policy which relates to interest rates

Who runs the economy?

No single person or institution is responsible, nor could they be, since economic activity is handled on a daily basis by millions of individuals and businesses. As far as any single body has responsibility for economic performance, though, it is the Treasury – the most important department in government.

The Chancellor of the Exchequer, the political head of the Treasury and usually the second most influential member of the government, is responsible for how much money the government takes through taxes, and how that money is spent. Government tax and spending currently accounts for around 40 per cent of the economy, so the decisions taken in the Treasury understandably have huge ripples out across the wider economy. The Chancellor also sets the inflation target for the Bank of England. Since the main way the Bank can meet this target is by raising and lowering interest rates, the Chancellor's inflation target has a big impact on interest rate movements.

What does the Bank of England do?

The Bank of England is the UK's central bank. It has a number of responsibilities, but only one really affects the way the political system works: setting the level of interest rates. The interest rate is the rate at which the Bank lends to other banks. To decide this rate, the governor and other members of the Monetary Policy Committee meet monthly to look at all the financial data and work out if they are on course to meet the government's inflation target. If not, they can use interest rates to rein in or stimulate economic activity (see box).

What happens when interest rates go...

. . . up?   Because it's more expensive to borrow money, the economy slows down, which causes inflation to fall.

The exchange rate rises, making British exports more expensive and making imports cheaper.

. . . down?   It's cheaper to borrow money, so people do, they spend it, and the economy grows, fuelling inflation (although inflation doesn't always keep rising when interest rates are low).

The exchange rate drops, making the pound less valuable compared to other currencies. British exports become more competitive in foreign markets and imports to Britain more expensive.

Because the interest rate level affects all kinds of other activities, the Bank is cautious about raising or lowering the rates. It's unusual to see rates rocketing up or dropping steeply; they usually change by a quarter of a percentage point.

This system was introduced soon after Labour came to power in 1997 by the Chancellor, Gordon Brown. Before then, decisions were taken by the Chancellor in consultation with the Governor of the Bank of England. Critics argued that under the old system the country's long-term economic prospects were often compromised in order to produce an election year boom. Brown's decision to give the Bank operational independence for interest rates was important because it took that power away from politicians.

How much tax does the government get?

The government gets about £500 billion from taxes a year (see Figure 10.1), and normally spends roughly the same amount – although there is almost always a gap between taxes and spending – either a deficit (too much spending) or a surplus (too much tax).

This level of taxation equates to about 40 per cent of the country's output or GDP. For the last couple of years, and for much of the previous century, it has spent slightly more than it has received, running a small deficit.

Because there is no right level for taxes, tax levels are set after a process of what amounts to economic and political guesswork.

Figure 11.1: Total government revenue, 2005/6

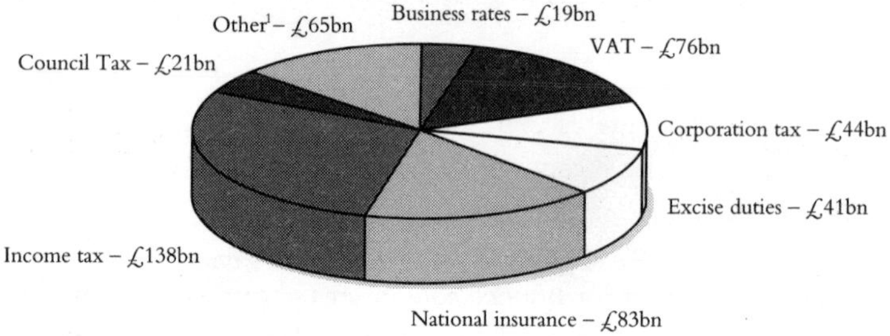

Other[1] – £65bn   Business rates – £19bn
Council Tax – £21bn   VAT – £76bn
Corporation tax – £44bn
Excise duties – £41bn
Income tax – £138bn
National insurance – £83bn

Notes
1. Includes capital taxes, stamp duties, vehicle excise duties, and some other tax and non-tax receipts (e.g. interest and dividends).
Source: HM Treasury. Crown copyright

Since taxes always slow the economy somewhat, they need to be high enough to pay for government spending, but not so high that they have a major impact on economic performance. But the effect of taxation will depend somewhat on what the money's being spent on: if it's all being re-circulated through spending on domestic projects, the economy will get a boost; if it's being used for debt repayment, in the short term it acts as a drag on the economy.

What is a stealth tax?

'Stealth tax' is a bit of an elastic phrase intended to beat the government over the head when it raises cash on the quiet with taxes such as that on pension funds. It's been used to cover all sorts of things which aren't really very stealthy at all – council tax, for example.

The more traditional split is between direct and indirect taxes. The former are taxes which are paid directly – for example income tax. Indirect taxes are not paid directly, but passed on by an increase in expenses – such as value added tax (VAT) on most goods. Most taxes are direct, with income tax the single largest source of income.

Should the government always balance its books?

There are different views on this, but many economists, and the government's own rules, say that it can borrow as long as it is for investment – on such things as new schools or roads – and doesn't just use it for its normal spending, for example on government services and paying wage bills.

The current government call this their 'golden rule': that over the 'economic cycle', the government can only borrow to invest. This is an important discipline, meaning that the government can't just run up huge deficits. They do it over the economic cycle so that they can borrow more in the bad years and repay more in the good years.

The problem with this rule is that it does depend on the inter-pretation of the economic cycle (the cycle runs from growth, through recession and back again to growth, and the cycles vary dramatically in length and intensity). So when the current Chancellor, Gordon Brown, formally changed the government's definition of the economic cycle in 2005, many critics saw it as a way of circumventing his own golden rule.

Of course, even if it meets the golden rule, it's never wise to borrow too much money. It will have to be repaid at some point, and the cost of the interest payments will be extremely large. What's more, if the government is borrowing very heavily over a long period, less money will be available for investment in private companies, making it harder for them to borrow, invest and grow.

Who does the government borrow money from?

When the government borrows money, it issues bonds – rather like giant IOUs – which are then bought and sold on the bond market. Mostly, they're bought by financial institutions – pension funds and investment houses – but individuals can also buy them, as can other countries' central banks.

It is also possible for countries to borrow from each other, or from the international financial institutions – the IMF and the World Bank. For example, on several occasions since 1945 Britain had to go cap in hand to the United States to ask for a loan to bail out our bad economy. In 1976, the government had the embarrassment of borrowing money from the IMF, an institution which Britain had helped set up and one which was more used to dealing with developing countries.

After the Labour government came to power in 1997, it chose

to use some of its normal income, and some unexpected cash gains, to pay back some loans, reducing the amount of money spent each year on interest payments.

How much does the government spend?

At the time of writing, the annual bill is about £500 billion, but that rises pretty much every year as a result of inflation and public and political pressure to spend more money on priority areas.

The majority of money is spent in a couple of areas – social protection (including tax credits, pensions and various types of benefit) and healthcare. Figure 10.2 shows the breakdown of spending in 2005/6.

Figure 11.2: Total government spending, 2005/6

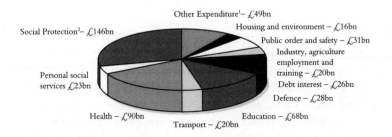

Other Expenditure[1]– £49bn

Social Protection[2]– £146bn

Housing and environment – £16bn

Public order and safety – £31bn

Industry, agriculture employment and training – £20bn

Personal social services £23bn

Debt interest – £26bn

Defence – £28bn

Health – £90bn

Education – £68bn

Transport – £20bn

Notes
1. Includes spending on general public services; recreation, culture, media and sport; international co-operation and development; public service pensions; plus spending yet to be allocated and some accounting adjustments.
2. Social protection includes tax credit payments in excess of an individual's tax liability.
Source: HM Treasury. Crown copyright

How is the money divided up?

This process is one of the most complicated and politically contentious in government. Different parties have had different ways of dividing up the cash, but the present government has a spending review every two to three years, in which it sets out the spending for the following three years.

The exact way in which the money is divided up is a political decision, taken jointly by the Treasury and the Prime Minister. Treasury ministers, and ultimately the Chancellor, will allocate the money based on the government's political priorities, and after representations from each government department and submissions from hundreds of outside bodies and thousands of individuals. This is then agreed with the PM. There are numerous balances to be struck and the views of different people and organisations will be weighted according to how powerful they are, how good their arguments are and so on.

To make sure that the money is spent properly, the spending reviews combine the announcement of the extra cash with what are known as PSAs (public service agreements). In effect, a PSA is a contract between the Treasury and a government department: if the Treasury gives the department a certain amount of cash, the department will do certain things in return. PSA is controversial because they give a great deal of extra power to the Treasury, allowing it to intrude into all sorts of aspects of what has traditionally been departmental business – the operation of government policy. While this is ostensibly to make sure the money is being spent properly, some people worry that it is really about handing more power to the Chancellor.

And these decisions are then announced in the Budget, are they?

Not necessarily. That's certainly the way it used to be – every year the Chancellor would announce what changes the government was planning to make to taxes, and how it would be dividing up the spending. However, since the introduction of spending reviews, not everything is announced in the Budget.

Nevertheless, the Budget still contains all the key decisions about tax, and because it is such an important part of the political calendar – and there's an element of political theatre about it – it still contains many spending decisions as well.

Booze and the Budget

The Budget is the only time when alcohol is allowed to be drunk in the House of Commons – the Chancellor is allowed to have a drink in his glass. This stems from the days of very long Budget speeches – in the nineteenth century they sometimes went on for five hours. These days, they're normally just a fifth of that.

Why privatise state companies?

Privatisation is the state selling off its assets. In Britain, most of the big privatisations happened during the 1980s, when the Conservative government felt the state owned too many companies. The sales included companies as diverse as British Airways, British Telecom and Rover.

Most of these companies had been nationalised over the previous fifty years – particularly in the immediate aftermath of the Second World War, when the Labour government felt state ownership was the best way of co-ordinating the economy's limited resources. Later nationalisations sometimes came about because companies got into economic difficulties and looked likely to go bust (for example Rolls-Royce in the 1970s).

The Conservatives wanted to privatise these companies because they believed the state's role in the economy should be cut back, but also because they believed the companies would flourish in the private sector. They argued that freeing them from political control and forcing them to operate in an open marketplace would allow them to become more efficient and provide better customer services. Many of the companies did become more efficient and more profitable.

This process benefited the government in three ways. First came the cash from selling the companies; second, they no longer had to stump up subsidies every year for companies which often lost a lot of money; third, as they became more efficient and more profitable, the privatised companies started paying large amounts of tax.

There are many critics, though, who often complain that hundreds of thousands of workers were sacked and worry about service quality. They point to companies such as Rover, which went bust in 2005, and argue that privatisation left the government unable to help when companies found themselves in difficulties.

The biggest privatisations since 1980

British Telecom (BT)

British Gas

BP

Regional electricity companies

Regional water authorities

Powergen and National Power

British Steel

Railtrack

British Airports Authority (BAA)
Rolls-Royce
Cable and Wireless
Britoil
British Airways (BA)
British Coal
British Aerospace (BAe)

Why get private companies to do what the government used to do?

For two main reasons. First, to have it done more efficiently. The argument goes like this: since a private company needs to make money, it will constantly be looking for ways to operate more efficiently, which isn't the case in the public sector. Critics of this 'contracting out' (handing contracts to bidders outside government) argue that the companies reduce standards to make their profits, and that the best-quality bid often isn't chosen because it's not always the cheapest.

The second rationale for involving private companies is when major investment is required. Handing the whole project to the private sector – particularly through a 'private finance initiative' (PFI) – allows the government to have something built without having to borrow all the money itself and pay the costs upfront. Instead, the money is gradually paid off over time. And since the government can't afford to stump up billions of pounds for hundreds of expensive projects all on day one, PFI effectively allows them to buy things on hire purchase and pay back the money gradually. Critics complain, though, that PFI projects are inflexible, expensive, and offer poor long-term value. They say the hire purchase costs outweigh the benefits.

> **Private finance in action: PPP for the Tube**
>
> The PPP (public–private partnership) for the London Underground is a classic example of an attempt to get lots of investment into the public infrastructure without all the money coming from government coffers. Its critics agree it's a classic example: but of a badly thought out political fudge which will end up costing more and delivering less.
>
> In 1999, the government decided the Tube needed improved signalling, upgraded stations and new trains – about £15.7 billion of investment over thirty years. Normally that money would have come directly from the government, through taxes or borrowing. However, it was decided to adopt the PPP to shift those costs away from central government.
>
> For the thirty-year life of the contract, the PPP hands control of the Tube's infrastructure to the private companies who are doing the work. Transport for London pays them what amounts to a service charge. In exchange, they are responsible for raising the investment capital themselves (like a giant bank loan), instead of just getting paid to do the work by the government. They must make the improvements during the contract period, with a panoply of checks to ensure they actually do it.

Why are companies always complaining about regulations?

Because regulations impose costs on companies which make them less competitive and mean they make smaller profits. That is seen as a bad thing because smaller profits mean people are less well rewarded for the risks they take, the government gets less money from taxes and ultimately some companies will go bust.

Not all regulations are bad, of course. Companies often support regulations which ban things giving their industry a bad name, or stop unfair competition from companies which cut corners.

It's the responsibility of politicians when introducing regulations to balance the expected costs against the projected benefits of the regulation. In the case of the national minimum wage, for example, many businesses (and politicians) predicted that thousands of jobs would be lost, but the government believed that the benefits would outweigh any potential problems (and in the event very few jobs were lost as a result).

Some businesses – usually smaller ones – are particularly affected by regulations and are particularly vociferous in their opposition. And costs can come from two directions – either directly (like the minimum wage), or indirectly through 'compliance costs'. It's the compliance costs which disproportionately affect small businesses. Because they don't have separate HR and accounts departments which can do the extra paperwork, other employees have to do it, taking up time which they'd otherwise use to earn money. Many regulations include opt-outs for small companies for just this reason.

What rights do unions have?

Unions are workers' organisations. In Britain they normally operate at three levels – in an individual company or workplace, at a national level in a particular industry, and at a general political level.

In the nineteenth century workers had to struggle for improved pay and workplace conditions, and the creation of unions was invaluable in improving the lives of millions of people. They became more powerful during the twentieth century and the bigger unions became politically powerful at every level. So much so, in fact, that by the 1970s many people considered them to have too much power, and the Thatcher government sharply curtailed their legal rights. Some of these were restored under the Labour government, but today union membership is much lower than it was at the height of union powers. They tend to be more influential in companies and industries where a majority of employees are members – like the FBU (Fire Brigades Union) in the fire service or the RMT (Rail, Maritime and Transport Union) on the London Underground.

Controversial issues about union powers and rights

Recognition	The right to be recognised by a company, if enough workers there vote for union recognition
Collective bargaining	The right to negotiate with a company on behalf of all union members in that company
Striking	The right for a worker to withdraw their labour if they're not happy with some aspect of their working conditions. There are strict rules about needing a vote before strike action
Secondary picketing	The right to strike in sympathy with employees of a different company
Political involvement	Many unions are affiliated with the Labour Party, giving them votes at the party conference and influence over the policy-making process, but there are rules about giving members' money to the party.

Does the government listen more to businesses or to unions?

The caricature of the Labour and Conservative Parties is that Labour governments are always in bed with their union paymasters while the Conservatives are in thrall to their business cronies. However, good governments listen to both, since both represent legitimate interests. And both spend a good deal of time and money trying to influence government.

Businesses have set up a number of organisations to represent them politically, although the best known are the CBI (Confederation of British Industry – mainly big companies), the Institute of Directors (for company directors) and the British Chambers of Commerce (more for small companies).

On the other side of the aisle are the unions. Unions used to represent people in particular sectors of the economy, such as the National Union of Teachers and the National Union of Mineworkers. These days, though, the big unions represent people from all corners of the economy. They have less political influence than they once did, largely as a result of wider changes in the economy.

How does globalisation affect British politics?

The main impact of globalisation is to increase international trade. Countries with low labour costs produce huge quantities of low-value manufactured goods for export. Because developed countries such as Britain do not wish to compete with these low-wage economies, most are attempting to turn themselves into economies which are based on research, technology, service industries and high-added-value manufacturing. This is certainly true in Britain, which is why all political parties emphasise employment and training to such an extent.

However, in many people's minds globalisation has negative connotations, because international trade is not conducted on an even playing field. Many of the richest countries impose tariffs (taxes) on imported goods, making it hard for poor countries to export their goods to them. This is done to protect domestic producers – for example American textile producers or French farmers. People in the developing world, though, find that while companies from rich countries gain access to their markets, there is little reciprocity in terms of access to markets in rich countries.

This affects British politics in a multiplicity of ways – from competition policy through trade policy to development and even education policy.

What's the difference between free trade and fair trade?

Free trade is trading between different countries in an open marketplace, without any unfair competition or support. If someone in Somalia produces a widget for £1 and it costs 20p to transport it to London, they can sell it for £1.20 (plus VAT). If it costs a British manufacturer £1.40 to make the same product, most people will be buying Somali widgets.

However, international trade often doesn't work in this way. In agriculture, for example, both the European Union and the United States subsidise their farmers heavily, and impose tariffs on producers from other countries. So if the Somali widget maker wanted to grow crops instead, she might find herself paying extra taxes and competing with British farmers whose crops were subsidised. Furthermore, some international companies use their power to buy products at very low prices, making it hard for many people in developing countries to make a decent living.

Fair trade is one alternative proposed by opponents of globalisation. They argue that people in rich countries should be prepared to pay more for goods, as long as the people who made them get the extra and can as a result afford a decent standard of living. Other critics of the current arrangements believe that the solution lies in eradicating tariffs and subsidies, and allowing everyone to compete fairly.

Where can I find out more?

I've tried to keep this book as simple as possible, on the basis that there's already enough waffle out there about politics to over-complicate it. However, not everything is over-complicated waffle, so for anyone who does want to find out more, here are some of my favourite resources. This isn't a comprehensive bibliography, but just a few books, magazines and websites which I find really useful.

Books

Who Runs This Place? by Anthony Sampson (John Murray), a brilliant general book about how Britain is run. It takes in the worlds of business and finance, as well as politics and the media.

The Prime Minister by Peter Hennessy (Penguin) is the best book on what a Prime Minister is expected to do, and how the various PMs since 1945 have done the job.

The Hidden Wiring, also by Peter Hennessy (Indigo), is an insightful and entertaining look at all the most important parts of the constitution. It's out of print, but is well worth getting hold of if you can.

This Blessed Plot by Hugo Young (Macmillan) is an excellent overview of Britain's relationship with Europe over the last fifty years.

A Special Relationship by John Dumbrell (Macmillan) is the best recent book about Britain's relationship with the United States. It manages to cover every angle and remain readable.

Britain in Numbers by Simon Briscoe (Politico's) is a brilliant book of facts about Britain.

The New British Politics by Ian Budge, Ivor Crewe, David McKay and Ken Newton (Longman) is the best textbook I've come across. It covers everything in this book, and much more.

Magazines

There are lots of political magazines. These are four I try to read regularly:
- The *New Statesman* is the main left-of-centre weekly.
- The *Spectator* is the main right-of-centre weekly.
- The *Economist* is a weekly news magazine. Its political coverage is excellent, but it covers much else besides. Its election time summaries are invaluable.
- *Prospect* is a monthly which offers a decent amount of space for its high-calibre contributors to develop their arguments: really good stuff.

Websites

- www.bbc.co.uk/news – a great resource for the latest stories and background about the news
- www.bbc.co.uk/actionnetwork – a great website for anyone wanting to get something done, be it at community level or nationally. It contains all sorts of resources, from 'how to' guides to ways of contacting people who've done similar things in the past
- www.epolitix.com – I love their daily e-mail summary of the political stories in the newspapers, with links to all the stories. If you don't have time to read a paper every day, this will give you the highlights
- www.guardian.co.uk – the best newspaper website in the UK, with everything in the paper, lots of detailed background reports and some web-only content
- www.locata.co.uk/commons – find out who your MP is.

Political parties

Don't be afraid to ask questions, particularly at election time. Election leaflets usually have a number you can call to speak to somebody locally, and some of the parties increasingly try to keep in touch with local residents between elections. You'd be amazed how few people show an interest, so if you do ask you may well get a proper answer.

If you aren't quite ready to face a politician yet, the party websites are pretty good, and at election time most newspapers and most political websites will have summaries of the manifestos and their own analysis of what the parties stand for. The main parties' websites are below, but it's just as easy to Google them.

- Conservatives: www.conservatives.com

- Labour: www.labour.org.uk
- Liberal Democrats: www.libdems.org.uk .

Radio

Today – from 6 a.m. to 9 a.m. on BBC Radio 4, Monday to Saturday, this is the best way of finding out what's happening in the world that day, and there's always a good dose of politics.

The Westminster Hour – Sunday evenings from 10 p.m. to 11 p.m. on BBC Radio 4. A good, detailed political programme.

Television

Daily Politics is one of my favourite political programmes. It's on BBC Two every day for half an hour at midday (Wednesdays 11.30 a.m.–1 p.m.)

The Politics Show – full disclosure, this is the programme I work for! It provides an excellent round-up of the week's politics as well as looking ahead to the next week. It's on BBC One at midday on Sundays.

This Week rounds up the week's politics with an imaginative approach. It's on BBC One on Thursdays at 11.35 p.m.

Index